Color Guide to
Steelhead
Drift Fishing

Bill Herzog

Frank
Amato
PORTLAND

Dedication

To my father and biggest fan, W.A. Herzog.

Acknowledgments

A sincere thank you to all the steelheaders who helped me become a drift fisherman: To Mike Draper and John Riedesel, top-notch guides who showed me the way; to Milt Keiser, Bill Luch and Jim Conway, three men with great pride in their chosen technique, who brought steelhead drift fishing to the masses; to Jed Davis and Bill McMillan, whose writings on steelhead behavior over the years added greatly to my streamside observations and to this book; to "The Doctor" for his years of inspiration; and always to the best fisherman I ever knew, Uncle Bob Pollen. Without his tutoring in my youth I would never have become a steelheader.

© 1994 Frank Amato Publications Inc.

Frank Amato Publications Inc.
PO Box 82112
Portland, Oregon 97282
(503) 653-8108

All photographs taken by author.

Book design and layout: Tony Amato

Softbound ISBN: 1-878175-59-9

UPC: 0-66066-00150-4

Printed in Hong Kong

10 9 8 7 6 5 4 3 2 1

CONTENTS

INTRODUCTION

Tap...tap...tap...the terminal gear bounces down the river, ticking bottom every few seconds through the holding water. Towards the end of the swing, just before you reel in and cast again, the offering stops and pulls ever so slightly. Instinct takes over. You strike hard and feel that unmistakable heavy head shake. Overdosing on adrenaline, you sprint down the gravel bank in hot pursuit of two and a half feet of chrome muscle that is determined to return to the ocean with you in tow. To over half a million anglers, this is drift fishing for steelhead.

Ever since the beginning of the twentieth century, when one of our forefathers discovered that a steelhead would strike a cluster of salmon eggs, drift fishing has been the most popular and effective technique for hooking steelhead trout. Just who this innovator was (he reportedly came from the Puget Sound region of Washington State, possibly either the Snohomish or the Puyallup river systems) is unknown. Back then, drift fishing for steelhead was an aberration. Fly fishing was the norm, and anglers only kept historical notes on fur and feathers. This is an interesting twist, as in modern times it is fly fishing for steelhead that is deemed eccentric, despite its growing popularity. Today, drift fishermen outnumber practitioners of all other steelheading techniques twenty to one. Whoever he (or she) was who first spooled braided silk lines onto a fly reel and started drifting bait, the door was opened to the most popular steelheading method of our time.

Personally, I will never forget the first steelhead I hooked on drift gear. After two unsuccessful seasons of four-times-a-week forays across the Tacoma Narrows Bridge to tiny Burley Creek, I was ready to bag the whole idea of ever making "the immaculate connection." Being able to see steelhead laying in the riffles and pools made it even more frustrating; obviously, I was doing something wrong. Now, I had hooked a few steelhead years before on a spoon by my uncle's guiding hand, but this drift fishing was brand new. I started reading books and articles in desperation, *Salmon Trout Steelheader* magazine in particular, and any article I could find by long-time Northwest outdoor writer Milt Keiser.

Between Milt's informative gospel on drift fishing and the many helpful articles on steelhead behavior in *STS*, it all came together on February 18, 1976. Without the help of expert steelheaders sharing their knowledge through books and articles, it would have been a lot longer before Number One hit the beach. This is my hope for this book: that the beginner takes this information and applies it streamside.

First, I want to make it clear that this book was written primarily for the beginner. Not that the experienced steelheader cannot also learn something. There are many tips and techniques for the veteran to pick and choose from; as well as several topics on drift fishing that have never found their way into "how to" books before. However, most information will be geared for newcomers.

Don't look for this book to be a "where to." You will not find listings of rivers or maps. The most popular rivers on the West Coast are already plugged with anglers during peak run times and do not need any more advertising. I mention a few rivers as examples, but nowhere will you see a map, any hint of access points or "hot spots." There are many smaller, less popular rivers and creeks that still hold fishable numbers of winter and summer steelhead. What it takes is time and exploration to find them. Maybe you have such a river in your collection. If not, put out some serious effort to find one of those uncrowded streams, or even a stretch of a popular river that receives little pressure, and learn it well. See it at all times of the year and at different volumes of flow. Learn run timings on the river. It will pay off for you with undisturbed steelhead and give you that bit of solitude every fisherman craves. When you find an out-of-the-way river or spot, guard its location and its fish. Only then can you really prac-

tice and refine these drift fishing techniques. I cherish my uncrowded water, and I know you will too.

Everything in this text was gathered from nearly two decades of drift fishing for steelhead: not just one man's findings and opinions (no steelheader is experienced enough), but rather a collection taken from encounters, articles, one on one talks and guide trips with the best steelheaders—plus thousands of hours of actual drift fishing time. Many have contributed to this text, all innovators in their own right. Some I have met, some I have not; some are great friends and lifelong fishing companions. Each has one thing in common: they love drift fishing for steelhead and have spent the better part of their lives honing and refining their chosen technique. Together they have contributed a treasure of information for this text. Thank you, gentlemen.

Guidelines here are West Coast in flavor. All the experience and guidelines I have gathered are from rivers in Washington, Oregon, British Columbia and California. I have had the opportunity to fish some of the finest rivers of the Great Lakes (Michigan streams in particular) but my experience with those localized techniques is limited, thus not quite qualifying me as "expert" enough to advise other anglers. Unless I have practiced the techniques and information and can attest to its effectiveness, you won't see it here. However, steelhead tend to behave the same under given conditions all over their range. These tips and techniques will help increase hookups for anglers wherever they pursue *Onchorhynchus mykiss*. Furthermore, every technique, rigging, drift lure, etc., within these pages has been thoroughly researched and proven.

Color Guide to Steelhead Drift Fishing covers a wide range of topics, all geared to increase the ratio of hours to hookups for the steelhead drift fisherman. Chapter One discusses winter and summer steelhead, their range and timing of runs, as well as characteristics of particular strains of fish, both native and hatchery. Chapter Two serves up the meat of the text: how to read water. You will learn how to recognize and identify holding water, how to find steelhead in any given piece of holding water at any time of year, plus how to find steelhead in the two most difficult types of water, tidal sections and canyons. Chapters Three and Four look at the full spectrum of drift fishing techniques and terminal riggings used to fish them, plus all the updated gear that has been absent in most drift fishing manuals until now. Chapter Five covers natural baits for steelhead and how to cure and care for them. Chapter Six shows you which outfit will match up with your drift fishing specifications, such as rods, reels, lines and other necessary personal gear. Lastly, we will show how to properly release a steelhead. Each fish shown in this book was carefully released alive.

I have been blessed to grow up and learn to drift fish for steelhead where it all began, in the Puget Sound area. From my home near Tacoma there are numerous winter and summer steelhead rivers no more that a few hours away, some only a few minutes away. Although they are not quite the steelhead factories they were when Willis Korf's Cherry Bobber and the Okie Drifter were the cutting edge of drift bobbers in the 1950s, there can still be good fishing at times. Suburban rivers like the Puyallup, Green, Skykomish and Snoqualmie still produce thousands of hatchery fish to Pugetropolis residents in early winter and summer. And if large, late natives are the quarry, the Olympic Peninsula has a half dozen big, brawling wild rivers that can truly test your mettle. If a fisherman wants to invest the time and skill, one of these coastal rivers of Indian legend can still produce a trophy at winter's end. On the horizon, there is the lorelei call of British Columbia. With countless steelhead rivers that never see more than a handful of anglers in a season, Canada is truly the last frontier. Now, with new regulations protecting wild fish and sound management of the resource, the future looks even brighter.

Steelheaders still have a great number of opportunities on a wide range of rivers. Learn to apply patience, persistence and confidence with this drift fishing knowledge, and they will open themselves up to you.

—*Bill Herzog,*
Federal Way, Washington.

CHAPTER 1

THE STEELHEAD: SEASONS, RANGE AND TYPES

1.) Winter Steelhead

If it's mid-November, take a peek outside your door at the foothills. Do you see some snow, perhaps a light dusting? Snow is the sign of a new beginning: the season of the winter run steelhead.

Although early November signals the beginning of the winter steelhead run in Washington State, each river system is inherently different when it receives the bulk of its fish. Here on the West Coast, run timing depends on several factors: geographic location, timing of hatchery and native runs, and to a lesser degree water temperature and volume.

Major rivers on the West Coast, primarily in Washington, Oregon and southern British Columbia, receive their runs of winter fish at two separate times, one early (November through January) and one late (February through April).

Intimately knowing the river you plan to fish helps in defining optimum fishing times during the peak of the run, and that includes choosing which type of winter steelhead you plan to target. The early runs are almost entirely hatchery fish, with some systems getting a mix of small numbers of early natives, while the late winter runs are predominantly wild steelhead, with a fraction of those being hatchery fish. To understand why hatchery and native steelhead return at different times of the winter season, we have to take a look at each one separately.

The differences between hatchery and native fish are run timing, physical appearance, amount of time that smolts (juvenile steelhead) spend in the rivers before traveling to salt, and, to some degree, aggressiveness and quality of fight.

First, let's take a look at hatchery steelhead. Thanks to a half century of hatchery research technology and advanced rearing procedures, smolts are fed diets and raised in warmer water conditions that grow them much larger and faster than juvenile fish in the wild. Because they are grown larger, they are released months earlier into their home rivers. Early released smolts mature faster, therefore returning a few months earlier than their native brothers. Late November, December and January are peak months for hatchery steelhead returns. The average hatchery winter steelhead will be smaller than natives, with most fish weighing between 6 and 10 pounds, these being two-salt fish, meaning two years spent in salt water before returning to spawn. This smaller size can be attributed to hatchery genetics, with the "cookie cutter" dimensions so familiar to fishermen that target early returning winter fish.

Some hatcheries, however, make serious efforts to take only the largest returning steelhead for their broodstock, the theory behind this being larger parents, larger offspring. This practice does result in some larger hatchery fish, with a greater number of three-salt fish weighing into the teens and more. For example, Washington's Cowlitz River receives hatchery fish that commonly weigh in the teens, and the Quinault Nation hatchery on the outlet of Lake Quinault plants fish that return in the high teens and low 20 pound range. Still, the majority of hatchery winter steelhead will be much smaller on the average than natives. Today, hatchery returns are unfortunately the bulk of winter steelhead in the Northwest. Hatchery steelhead make up 70% of the runs in Washington's coastal rivers, 80% of the runs in lower Columbia tributaries, and 65% of winter fish in Oregon coastal streams.

Hatchery steelhead also differ greatly in physical appearance. The easiest way to identify a hatchery fish is by the condition of its fins. By growing up in confined hatchery pond, some of the fins will be bent and deformed. The rays in the anal and dorsal fins will be crooked and ragged looking. Tips of the tails, top and/or bottom, will be rounded. The Washington Department of Wildlife clips off the adipose fin (the fleshy, tiny fin between the dorsal and the tail) on hatchery smolts for positive identification on adult fish. A number of other states and Canada are now fin-clipping steelhead also. Fin clipping allows an angler to immediately identify a hatchery fish from a wild one.

Cold weather means heavy jackets, wool gloves, neoprene waders—and winter steelhead, such as this bright February native held by the author.

Native winter steelhead are a contrast to hatchery steelhead. Naturally produced fish take longer to grow to smolt stage. Whereas juveniles in a hatchery take about a year to grow before release, in the wild it takes two to four years. Native fish are later running, but not quite as predictable as hatchery fish. Native steelhead will overlap the hatchery run in November, December and January, with many rivers receiving the majority of their natives during these months. Again, it has everything to do with each individual river system and strain of steelhead determining peak run timing. In general, the majority of Washington, Oregon and southern British Columbia streams receive their native runs in February, March and April.

The native winter steelhead's physical appearance is striking. Nowhere on the adult native's body can you find evidence of having bounced off the walls of a concrete rearing pond. Instead of deformed or missing fins, a native will have straight rays and no fin clips. The dorsal will be tall and pointed, and so will the tips of the tail.

Not only is the native steelhead more captivating to the eye, they have several other qualities that are held in the highest esteem by fishermen. Those qualities are size, aggressiveness and fight. Native steelhead generally are larger, perhaps because on large, brawling rivers, only the largest and strongest fish can navigate successfully. In the ten-thousand years since the glaciers receded, some rivers fitting this description have become famous for giant, late winter trophies of 20 pounds or more, such as the Olympic Peninsula's Queets, Hoh, Quinault and Quillayute rivers. The quality that produces large native steelhead is the same that creates superior fighters, and makes them more aggressive to lures. The unbending will and strength required for survival in the wild simply cannot be reproduced in a hatchery pond. Wild winter steelhead are better biters—that's a fact. Why this is so is anyone's guess, but again the fish's origins must play a significant part.

Whether hatchery or native, when a winter steelhead first enters fresh water, it is at its pinnacle of beauty: gun metal blue/black back, sharply separated at the lateral line by bright silver sides leading down to a stark white belly. Even the tail has streaks of silver on its rays. Winter steelhead tend to return to their rainbow coloration after a few days to a week in fresh water. Males color up faster than females, the bucks first getting a pink/red on the gill plates, with a matching color stripe along the lateral line to the tail after a few days in the home river. Females stay brighter longer: only after a few weeks do they start to get rose-colored like the bucks. All winter steelhead enter rivers sexually mature. Even bright fish are egg or milt heavy, because spawning is only days to a few months away. Regardless of when winter fish enter their home rivers, early or late, the majority will spawn in late winter to early spring.

2.) Summer Steelhead

The greatest diversity when steelhead fishing is encountered during summer. In one season, you can find yourself in a pair of shorts, waist-deep in 63 degree water under a blazing 90 degree sun, while three months later you might be bundled in six layers of wool and neoprene waders, chest-deep in 38 degree water in a howling snowstorm. In the desert. In the rain forest. On the coast, or four hundred miles from it inland. Every scene has the same common denominator: summer steelhead.

Due to warmer water and a high percentage of body fat, summer steelhead are aggressive, acrobatic and more exciting to hook than winter fish.

Summer steelhead enter West Coast rivers as early as March and as late as November. Despite this wide variance, the bulk or peak of most runs occurs from May through July, although some streams don't see the largest concentrations of fish until September and October. As when fishing for winter steelhead, intimately knowing the river(s) you have chosen to fish will determine peak run timing and best fishing. Because some summer steelhead spend up to a year in fresh water, they are loaded with extra fat, giving them a thicker look across the back than their winter relatives. Whereas a winter fish looks deeper in the belly due to maturing egg skeins and milt filling the body cavity, a fresh summer run will have a leaner look, almost as if it was spawned out. A summer steelhead's eggs and milt are still tiny and undeveloped.

The early summer steelhead, or "springer," is truly the greatest prize of the year. These are mostly native fish, born of rivers with numerous falls, rapid drops and difficult-to-reach canyons that are perfect areas for holding, spawning and smolt rearing.

Non-glacial streams normally run low, clear and warm during the summer months. Mike Cronen matched a light action rod with six-pound line to bring this Vancouver Island summer run to hand.

Their shaded pools stay cool and oxygenated during even the warmest months. Early native spring runners are exceptionally beautiful—thicker across the back and much brighter than other season steelhead. They are a midnight blue, almost black from head to tail, with brilliant silver and bright white sides and belly. These fish can, and often do, jump numerous times at eye-level when hooked, a trait that comes from thousands of years of genetics. Natural selection has chosen only the strongest leapers, the ones able to successfully hurdle high falls and chutes common to their home streams.

Rivers like the Queets, Hoh, Dungeness, Dosewallips, Duckabush and Skokomish on the Olympic Peninsula have small runs of these early native summer fish, as does the Washougal, East Fork Lewis, Kalama and Wind, tributaries of the lower Columbia. These rivers all share a common feature: they have canyon stretches and receive snow melt in late spring and early summer that contributes to increased flows. This is the main theory behind the early returning "springer:" the increased flows make for easier passage over obstructions such as falls and chutes. This augmentation of water is rarely present during the dry periods of July and August. These early runs are now protected in Washington State by mandatory release laws for all native (non-fin clipped) summer steelhead. They deserve their wild, protected status. On the end of a fishing line they are matchless.

Take nothing away from the summer steelhead that come into their home rivers later than the "springers". Add warmer water conditions, higher percentage of body fat, and the fact that summer runs do actively feed while in the rivers and you come up with a fish that has speed and acrobatic agility a step higher than its winter cousin.

While summer and winter steelhead generally share the same rivers and spawning areas, there are some runs that differ greatly.

These are true summer runs; they must sometimes travel hundreds of miles inland to eastern Washington, eastern Oregon, Idaho and deep into British Columbia. By virtue of the great distances these fish must travel and the time it takes for them to reach their destination, they have zero competition for spawning areas from winter steelhead. It takes these special fish sometimes three to six months to arrive at their home waters.

Their long, arduous upstream odyssey has produced some strains that are the most impressive steelhead known for size, strength and physical appearance. The two notable river systems that host these trophies are the Columbia (Snake, Clearwater and Salmon rivers) and the huge Skeena River in northern British Columbia. While it is commonly believed that late, native winter steelhead are the largest to be found, these two river systems are the producers of the true giants. The Columbia's Clearwater River has its noted "B" run of hatchery supplemented fish that commonly run high teens to mid-twenties, but it is the Skeena that is champion. Rivers with names like Bulkley, Kispiox, Babine and Sustut produce native steelhead in the 20 pound range, with some much heavier. Dozens of fish from 30 to 35 pounds have been landed in these rivers since their discovery in the 1950s. The Babine and Kispiox, however, produce the real monsters. The all-tackle world records are from these rivers: 33 pounds on a fly (Kispiox) and 38 pounds on a spoon (Babine). Native Americans who net fish from these rivers have taken some steelhead weighing over 40 pounds. During a trip to the Skeena in 1987, a year of exceptionally sized fish, I heard of one male steelhead of 52 pounds taken in October in a Babine Indian weir. Imagine *that* on the end of your rod! These magnificent fish deserve our respect and admiration and should always be released. Other rivers that support runs of long-distance summer steelhead are the John Day, Methow, Grande Ronde, Deschutes and Klickitat rivers in

Washington and Oregon, and the huge Thompson River in British Columbia.

Summer steelhead, unlike their winter relatives, will feed while in their home rivers, specifically at two different times. The first feeding stage is when the steelhead enters the river. For the first few weeks in fresh water the summer steelhead will eat anything aquatic or terrestrial it can find, then it will start to feed again in late autumn before winter holdover. While summer steelhead do not search for food while in the river, they will feed if the opportunity presents itself. Autopsies of hatchery summer fish, by the author and many others, have found these delicacies in steelhead stomachs: large nightcrawlers, beetles, hellgrammites, caddis larvae, grasshoppers, tadpoles, salmon eggs, water ouzels (small, black diving birds about the size of a sparrow) and caps from ball point pens! Summer steelhead do not have to feed, however, the summer run has all the body fat it needs to over-winter without eating.

Wild summer steelhead in Washington and Oregon are the minority compared to hatchery fish. The Skamania strain of hatchery fish, descended from wild Wind and Washougal River summer runs, have been planted extensively in Washington, Oregon, Northern California and the Great Lakes. Although inferior to wild steelhead due to extensive interbreeding, Skamania hatchery fish have provided summertime fisheries where there were none previously, or unfishably small numbers. These hatchery fish have spawned successfully in some rivers.

It may be late autumn, and there may be snow on the ground, but native Skeena River steelhead are true summer fish. They must travel hundreds of miles to reach their spawning grounds.

CHAPTER 2

READING WATER AND DECODING RIVERS

Every steelheader has his favorite technique, one preferred over all others. Take a look at some of the current experts: Bill McMillan and Jim Teeny, masters of the fly rod; Buzz Ramsey and Clancy Holt, peerless when drift fishing and backtrolling; Jim Bedford and Jed Davis, the undisputed gurus of spinner fishing—each prefers to fish for steelhead his own way, and each method is completely different from the other. Each of these individuals is quite capable of hooking numbers of steelhead that could range into the hundreds in one year, at a time when such numbers seem impossible to come by. Any of these men, if made to switch techniques with one of the others, would in time after becoming comfortable with his new technique do equally as well. Why? Regardless of how they choose to fish, each has the same time honored talent: they are scholars of the school of reading water which is the one true key to steelheading success.

Fishermen place too much emphasis on boats, rods, lures, colors and so on. Gear and all the accessories receive too much credit for hooking steelhead. A fellow with dull hooks, an old glass rod and rotten salmon eggs will outfish the "dude" with top-notch, state-of-the-art gear if he has more skill at reading water. It's true. Matching terminal drift gear in size and color does play a significant part in consistently hooking steelhead, but not as important a part as knowing where in the river the fish will be.

This chapter is about reading water. Not technique, not terminal gear and not baits—that will be covered in later chapters. The following tells you how to find steelhead in their environment by dealing with structure, water temperature, time of year, water volume and clarity and rivers by sections. It will show you how to analyze and recognize, and using step by step evaluation be able to employ your drift techniques and hook fish.

1.) Recognizing and Identifying Holding Areas

The first step in reading water is realizing that no two sections of river are the same. With this in mind, how do you go about generalizing what holding water should look like? There are several keys to physical makeup of river contours that identify possible holding areas. I say "possible" because often, upon closer inspection, what first appears to be steelhead water fails to meet holding water standards.

In a typical free-flowing, fast, steep gradient western steelhead river, you can eliminate 70% of the river proper as possible holding areas. We can make a list of areas that do not hold fish, and they are common to the physical makeup of western streams. Waterfalls, chutes, rapids and wide, steep shallows (two feet deep or less) are all too swift and powerful, or, in the case of the shallow wide drop, too fast and with no cover to house resting steelhead. This leaves 30% of the river with areas that might hold steelhead. The word "resting" is the solution to where to start looking for holding water on rivers.

"Comfort" may be a good word to use also; you will never find the silver ghost laying over any type of sand bottom. Sand and fish gills do not mix, and steelhead avoid these sandy areas, even though a spot may look like holding water. If the bottom is predominantly sand, skip it. Gravel, rocks and boulders comprise the bottom makeup to look for. Steelhead will lay on top, along side and behind rocks. Rocks and boulders also help break up current, making it easier for fish to hold without expending energy. When the river flows over a submerged large rock or boulder, it causes a swirling boil, giving away a prime holding location.

Steelhead are looking specifically for spots that can give them rest and safety from predators. Since they use the path of least resistance when seeking holding areas, you must look to areas where the river begins to slow and gain depth. This slower area must meet a set of ground rules.

Steelhead gravitate toward quieter, flowing water (a man's casual walking speed is a good gauge) near the bottom of a river that ranges from 3 to 15 feet deep. There are exceptions to this depth (see Tidewater and Canyons later in this chapter), but for 95% of any river you will fish, these depths are written in stone. These deeper areas can be any size and length, depending on the size and physical makeup of each individual river. These areas have many names, but we can break them down into four specific sections as they take form below the falls, rapids and chutes.

RIFFLE: The area where rapid, crashing water first starts to slow down. The riffle is characterized by bouncy, choppy water caused by refracting off rocks and small boulders (the same kind that attract steelhead) as the water slows. Riffles are commonly 2-1/2 to 6 feet deep.

POOL: Often the deepest portion of holding water, this is the area where the riffle begins to calm down. Bouncy chop is replaced by undulating slicks and boils. Pools can be anywhere from a few feet deep in the smallest streams, to several fathoms in large rivers, but commonly range from 5 to 20 feet deep.

TAILOUT: Where the depth of the pool gradually lessens, shallows up and is, to a degree, wider than the rest of the holding area. The tailout is literally the tail-end of a classic piece of steelhead holding water.

BREAK: The point directly after the tailout where the holding water shallows and speeds up to again form a rapid, falls or a chute. The "pool" is normally the largest portion of the holding water, but that is a generalization. Some stretches of holding water are nothing more than a riffle before the break.

This brings us back to that small percentage of water on any river that consistently holds fish. The "riffle-pool-tailout" configuration makes up 40 to 50% of the physical makeup of a typical western steelhead river. If this is all potential holding water, where does the small percent come in? It brings us to the most important factor in reading steelhead holding water, and that is finding the "flat spots."

Veteran steelheaders all have a favorite run that consistently gives up strikes. There may be other runs or stretches of holding water near that look the same, but rarely produce like the favorite hole. Beginners take note. Sherlock Holmes said, "We see, but we do not observe." The reason for the one run producing well over the others can be attributed to the river bottom actually being flat, or without any downward (seaward) slope. Remember, no two stretches of holding water are alike; "flats" can be 2 to 200 feet long. These flat spots are areas of holding water that actually go up; that is the river bottoms are ever so slightly tilted upward. In

the classic holding water situation of "riffle-pool-tailout," this is common where the pool transforms to tailout. At this point, the bottom is sloped upward. The upward slant to the bottom provides steelhead with the easiest resting area due to the slower, refracted current. The flats, however, can occur anywhere in the river where there is sufficient cover for holding fish. The start of the tailout is an obvious flat area, but flats can be found in long riffles; deep troughs that extend for 100 yards; deep runs; along side back eddies; along clay ledges and even behind large boulders that are situated inside chutes and rapids.

To find a flat spot in a section of holding water, simply study the bank on the opposite side of the river, focusing on the water line. Follow the contour of the water line as the run progresses downstream. You will notice that these holding spots will slope downward, then at some point will "flatten" out and flow level. Some stretches may even seem to tilt upward. These are the key spots to concentrate on when reading water. Some fishy-looking beats may have more than one flat spot. Some may have none, and these "flatless" places, even though they may look like practical holding areas, are usually the ones that are vacant. But remember, these flats are not always a gimme, just like every other aspect of learning to read water, there will always be variables. Every river and season has conditions where steelhead will be found in other portions of definable holding water. Locating the flat areas on rivers is still the most important first step in identifying holding water.

When deciphering a river, if you can safely wade across or take a driftboat, look at the holding water from both banks. What may look at first glance from one side as "too fast" or "frogwater" (too slow) may qualify as ideal holding water when viewed from the other bank. Currents can be deceptive, and just because it did not fish well from one side due to a number of factors (such as converging currents, back eddies or just the necessity of a longer cast) does not mean a piece of water is incapable of holding steelhead. It may have less (or more) current that could suit a migrant's taste, and could even have a small "flat."

One more point to ponder. Steelhead, when moving upriver, always follow the path of least resistance. In normal to low water, this equates to travel in the portion of the river with the greatest flow. The increase of water allows easier passage for fish over boulders, rapids, chutes and obstructions. There is always one side of the river that has more flow. This is a major key when trying to determine which side of the river steelhead will choose to hold. Most of the time this is fairly simple; the deepest or slowest portion (more suited to hide steelhead) of the river is on one side. There are times when they are difficult to tell apart. It can sometimes be imperceptible, such as a casual glance at a wide, smooth tailout. The flow may look even all the way across. However, how many times have you waded three-quarters of the way across these tails only to find, in the last few feet, the flow was just a bit stronger and the water just a bit deeper? You have just found the side of the holding water the steelhead will travel through, and the side they will hold in.

How can you determine the side with the most volume? This is something that can come only from close observation, which in turn comes from experience. This is evident when a pool forms two nearly identical slots below a rapid or riffle. You will notice (especially if the river is heavily fished) that even though both edges of the pool look similar, one side produces 90% of the fish. While the other non-productive side may look just as good, it is more than likely missing key ingredients for holding steelhead. Upon closer examination, these sides are sloped (not flat, like the other side), have less flow and may have fewer rocks and boulders with more sand.

Like all other bits and pieces of reading water and steelhead behavior, there are no "exacts" when locating fish. All the points Mentioned thus far deal with low to above moderate river flow. When rivers are high and off color, the rules change. (See Part Two: Finding Steelhead.) These are, however, the basic ground rules to recognizing and identifying holding areas.

2.) Finding Steelhead By Water Height, Temperature and Degrees of Visibility

In this portion of the chapter, we will not be discussing summer and winter steelhead separately. Even though they are completely different species that enter a wide range of river systems at varying times of the year, they share a common behavioral trait. Steelhead, no matter if they are winter, spring or summer fish, all respond to water temperature, height and clarity the exact same way. If you were to take a late February native winter run and an early August hatchery summer run and drop them into a 50 degree river, they would both gravitate to the same holding spot and strike the same lure. Therefore, every generalization applies to the current conditions encountered by fishermen on the river at that time of year.

The "big three"—height, temperature and clarity—are the keys to finding steelhead. Earlier we discussed how to identify holding areas. Now we have to look at water height along with water temperature to understand steelhead behavior. We will apply the variables that will help pinpoint holding locations in riffles, pools, tailouts, etc. Keeping in mind that water temperature is the major factor in finding steelhead in holding water, the most important purchase you can make is a water thermometer. Taking a temperature reading before you fish (it only takes a few minutes) makes the following a helpful guide to find fish, thus practically eliminating guesswork.

These variables apply only to medium to large rivers. Small streams ("small" meaning unfloatable with a drift boat, or any smaller water that is 10 to 15 feet across) are a different story altogether and will be covered later in this chapter.

The first condition is one that no steelheader likes to deal with, but it is an unfortunate reality, especially in the rainy, wet Northwest in late fall, winter and spring. High, brown, almost flood stage water causes steelhead to react the same way, regardless of water temperature. Heavy flows will make 95% of the river too fast for fish to rest in. The only areas slow enough for steelhead in high water are normally right next to the bank in the lower end of holding water, usually close to a former tailout. At first glance a high, dark roaring river is quite intimidating and normally cold, from 38 to 48 degrees, with 6 inches—give or take a few—of visibility. In this condition steelhead will search out the slowest water they can find. This slow, next-to-the-bank water is a degree less roily, therefore having less gill-clogging silt than the heavy flows. The slower water is often one to a few degrees warmer than the main flow. These are the easiest, most comfortable areas for steelhead to rest in during adverse conditions.

These high, dark water areas are not very wide, usually one to 3 feet. At the edge of the slow water, there will be a "parting" or "transition line" (you will see these terms again), where fast water meets slow. Here, within a foot of this parting line, is where steelhead will lay. If the slow water is more than 4 feet

This 12 lb. Olympic Peninsula winter run was hooked in a slow current edge in 36 degree water. A #6 Spin-n-Glo provided a large profile in tandem with action to provoke the strike.

The drift fisherman averages one steelhead for every six hours of probing water. Patience paid off for this angler with a spring native.

change its position in the river due to rapid increase of water volume, it will become timid and non-receptive. Keep a close watch on river levels before you travel to fish. Again, rapidly rising water will turn off steelhead. If you still want to fish high, off-colored rivers, there are a few techniques that will produce steelhead under impaired visibility conditions. (See Chapter Three: The High Water Solution.)

Now we will factor in water temperatures, apply each set of temperatures to the different phases of fishable water height and clarity, and see how a steelhead reacts to each set in its holding area.

33 to 38 degrees: Steelhead in these extremely cold conditions are going to be lethargic, with all upstream movement ceasing until warmer water conditions prevail. Water this cold, with very few exceptions in glaciated rivers, will always be clear with 6 feet to unlimited visibility. It is in these temperatures that steelhead are found in the slowest and deepest water. In this slow water, where there is limited oxygen, the fish's metabolism has slowed down to the point of minimal oxygen needs. The slow water, on the edge of a faster flow, best suits the frigid water dwellers. The deeper holes, from 4 to 10 feet deep (the slowest portion of this deeper water), are normally a degree or two warmer than the faster flows. A good example of this type of water is the inside area of a corner hole, where the river makes a 90 degree turn against a ledge or wall. This slow water on the inside is an ideal spot to find fish. Steelhead will gravitate toward the warmer, quieter water where they are more comfortable. Angling in these icy flows is questionable. Steelhead can still be caught, but the fish's lower metabolism substantially reduces their quality of fight. Even though the water is clear, steelhead will still stay out of the faster holding water and lay in the slow, deep water on the edges of the current.

40 to 44 degrees: This temperature is still on the cold side, and steelhead will tend to stay in the slower water on the current edges. This is also the temperature you will commonly find during most of the winter season (November through mid-March) on Northwest steelhead rivers, and the point on the thermometer where fish will start to move. Steelhead, along with showing signs of upstream movement, will start to become aggressive to bait and lures. Fishing now becomes tricky. Even though you will be concentrating on slow edges, deep smooth runs and transition water, in clear conditions of maximum visibility steelhead may be also found in choppy runs of moderate depth. When water conditions allow (more than 2 feet of visibility), it pays to work everything from tailouts to the head-ins. All flat spots that qualify as holding water can hold fish in these temperatures.

45 to 50 degrees: These are winter-type temperatures, but they can happen on Northwest rivers anytime from March into June, depending on river location and if it has any glacial origin. In these temperatures steelhead start to show the greatest

deep, steelhead might lay there, but try and avoid it for two reasons. One, in cloudy, roily water with severely limited visibility, light penetrates weakly or not at all. Conditions like this with less than a foot of visibility, available light—depending on time of day and amount of direct sunlight—will penetrate 2 or 3 feet of water. By staying shallow, you are able to use all available light in finding and hooking off colored water steelhead. The second reason for avoiding slow water more than 4 feet deep is that steelhead will gravitate toward the shallows anyway. The cloudy color of the dark water gives them a sense of security, and there is much less silt in the shallower, calmer water. Try to avoid these conditions, for they are difficult to fish. This formula for finding high water steelhead only works when the river height has stabilized, or is no longer rising. Remember, steelhead normally will only be aggressive when the water height is stable or dropping. (Author's note: I have seen steelhead strike aggressively in rising water on some Vancouver Island streams.) When a steelhead is forced to increase in activity. Quality of fight in the fish is upgraded because of the warmer water, and they will also move freely upriver. In this temperature range, fish will start to gravitate to the areas of holding water with more flow; for instance, the breaks at the ends of tailouts, to the slightly faster water on the inside of current breaks or parting lines, and choppy runs in the main portion of the flats. In this range you will find steelhead from 3 to 10 feet deep, depending on prevailing lighting conditions and water clarity. At this temperature range and above, where steelhead will hold in a flat depends upon how bright the day is. While fish will still hold in the deeper, slower, smooth water they will retreat to the holding areas with the broken surface for more cover. While steelhead may be negotiated anywhere on cloudy days during average water flow and color, warmer water makes fish more sensitive to light, and sunny days dictate you must now work the areas that have the most surface cover.

51 to 60 degrees: These temperatures represent the steelhead's maximum activity range. Now is when fish respond best to lures and drift gear and show fighting credentials the proudest. These are the typical temperatures you will find in glaciated and non-glacial rivers from April to September, earlier or later depending on how warm the weather may be. In these conditions, steelhead will always lay in the "meat" of the holding water, or areas with substantial flow and cover. The deeper, slower sections that held fish in colder conditions will now be void. Warmer water means less dissolved oxygen in slower sections, so fish will seek out flats with a broken, choppy surface, normally 3 to 7 feet deep. This broken water contains more oxygen. Steelhead holding in these temperature ranges are now more light affected than at any other time. Time of day also dictates where in the holding water you will find them. Let's assume, for these temperature ranges, that the weather will be fairly warm during the day. To see how steelhead react to lighting, we have to break down periods of the day and different lighting conditions.

From early morning (crack of dawn) until the sun comes over the hills or treetops, lighting will be lowest; the majority of the steelhead will be laying in slightly deeper water (3 to 6 feet) with a choppy or broken surface. From the time in late morning when the sun hits the water to mid-day or early afternoon, maximum light will be on the river, causing fish to move into the shallower portion of the holding water with the greatest amount of broken surface. These areas are commonly the fast riffles at the top end of the flat section, after the termination of a rapid or chute.

When fishing cloudy days in these water temperatures, steelhead will behave the same, although you can find them in a wider range of holding water. After dawn breaks to early morning, even under cloudy cover, they will still move up into the areas of broken holding water. However, you will still find them in slightly deeper, broken surface areas down into the pool, as long as there is no direct sunlight.

61 to 65 degrees: This is the top end of the temperature scale you would want to fish. Oxygen levels in river water this warm are dangerously low for steelhead. The only areas where you will find fish in these conditions are in the shallow (2-1/2 to 4 feet deep), broken riffles where the river bed starts to flatten after a chute or rapid. This is the only area in the river that contains enough dissolved oxygen for steelhead to be comfortable. In water temperatures higher than 66 degrees, steelhead are fighting to live. At these extremes fish will cease movement and "bury" themselves in a section of holding water and wait for cooler temperatures. Releasing a steelhead under these stressful conditions is no longer an option; they are difficult if not impossible to revive

after expending themselves in the warm water.

Now that steelhead behavior has been determined by water temperature, let's look at how water height and clarity affects their choice of holding areas. When you combine water temperature with degrees of height/clarity, steelhead behavior is definitely easier to understand.

Since holding behavior in high, roily, dark water conditions has already been discussed, the following will focus on the fishable stages ("fishable" meaning any degree of visibility of 12 inches or more, this is the amount of visibility when drift gear becomes a feasible method of hooking steelhead) of a typical West Coast steelhead river after it starts to retreat from the high, brown, near-flooding stage.

When steelhead rivers first begin to drop away from the high stage and become fishable, color and water flow will still be substantial. This is the point where steelhead will begin to move freely upriver. The high, but not too high, volume of water allows them easier passage upstream around obstacles. Water color will normally be brownish green to whitish green. With increased flows and dark, restricted visibility, steelhead hold in the edges of the current in the slower water. These slow edges are always right against the bank, and commonly near tailout portions of the flat holding water. After negotiating heavy rapids and chutes, these sections are typically the first portions of flat, holding type water they rest in. They cannot fight the heavier currents in the main flow of the river, and the dark color of the water gives them security in the shallower, calm edges. Here they also escape lingering silt, though it is not as bad as when the water was higher and roily brown.

Dropping from the fishable foot of visibility to approximately 2 feet of visibility, there will still be considerable flow, but substantially less than during the previous stage. Water color in this stage is commonly white/green to emerald, or the "drool" stage that every fisherman learns to love after waiting several days after a heavy rain blew the river out. This means the tight edges of slower water are now measured in feet, with the smooth, moderate depth runs (4 to 7 feet deep) and tailouts especially being the prime target areas. The dark green hue to the water provides steelhead with a sense of security; they will lay in shallower tailouts and calm edges under the canopy of color. They do not yet feel the need to move to deeper, heavier flowing water for cover. While this may be the best water condition to drift fish for steel-

Steelhead will seek out portions of the river that provide rest and cover. Because of unlimited visibility, this summer run was laying in a broken, choppy riffle.

head, you should never restrict your trips to rivers only during these times. Learning steelhead behavior on local streams can only be done thoroughly if they are fished at other than optimum conditions.

When the river drops again from the "classic" green canopy of color to the next stage (3 to 5 feet of visibility), the changes in steelhead behavior are immediately apparent. The fish no longer feel safe in shallower water because the green color has, for the most part, left. This makes the tailouts and edges that held steelhead in the slightly higher water now void. The river does, however, still hold a tint of color and has a ways to go before being classified as low and clear. What has happened is that the fish have moved into the deeper holding water, preferring areas where the bottom is just barely visible to where the whitewater at the top end of the pool stops and starts to flatten out. Steelhead at this stage are still on the move and easily fished for. This is a better condition to fish in than the "just dropped into shape green" discussed a bit earlier. With the increased visibility, a drift fisherman can work flat spots more quickly, the clearer water allows the steelhead to see a larger area, thus reqiring fewer casts to work a section of holding water. The river still has some color, and in the deeper, choppy spots the fish, still feeling secure, will be aggressive.

When rivers continue to drop and reach the final stage of low flows, steelhead will be found in two areas, depending on time of year, or more specifically on water temperature. The water will now have 6 feet or more visibility, and fish will again move to find security and comfort. With minimal flows and unrestricted visibility, steelhead will be at the very beginning of the holding water, where the rapid or chute empties into the riffle. This broken water is their only cover in the skinny flows and provides more oxygen. The exception is that when the water is below 44 degrees, you will still find them in deep water of 15 feet or less, where the bottom is not readily visible. In colder flows, there is less need for oxygen because the steelhead's metabolism slows. Even though the water is low, continue to look for the flats, even

in the broken, riffled water at the head-ins to holding areas.

Remember, a water thermometer is the drift fisherman's best friend. Water temperature when matched up with water height and color will tell you with accuracy every time all through the year where steelhead will hold in medium to large rivers.

Once you master these skills, you will have 90% of the knowledge needed to consistently hook fish.

Medium sized and larger rivers can have a myriad of variables for consistently finding steelhead. Small streams and rivers have only a short set of rules for finding fish and are simple to decode. Run timing is still all-important, and water temperature plays a part in upstream movement of fish. But that's where the similarities to larger water end.

A small stream/river by definition is water that is too small to even consider floating in any craft, even the smallest mini-drifters and rafts. A small steelhead stream can be waded just about anywhere, except in the highest of water conditions. Because of their diminutive size, fish are easier to find for a few reasons. One, their shorter length means steelhead will not be as scattered. This requires less water to probe in a day's fishing to get a hookup. The second reason is the ticket for reading small streams: steelhead are easier to find in small water because their choices for holding water is limited to any piece of water that is large enough to hide them. This is why in small streams, it is possible to hook a steelhead laying over a moderately sandy bottom, or in a non-flat area. Rarely are holding spots over 10 feet in length. Small water steelheading is not practiced in deep runs, riffles and pools, but more likely in pockets. Concentrate fishing efforts near boulders, downed trees, undercut banks, culverts, mini-waterfalls, sweeper tree branches on the surface of the water and especially the rapid head-ins of pools. Water temperature plays almost no factor in finding holding spots in small water, as any place that looks like one of the previously mentioned areas that could be large enough to hide a 6 pound fish, probably is.

As you work the pockets of a small stream, keep asking yourself, "Does this spot have enough cover to hide a fish?" Visualize where a steelhead might lie. It's important to fish everything, even spots that may look marginal. They may be deeper or larger than they appear. Be sure to wear polarized glasses. They will help you pick out underwater obstructions, aid you in finding fish and keep your drift gear free of unseen snags hidden by the glare. Always wear dark clothing. You will normally be very close to the target water and to the fish.

When small streams run high and a bit off-color (they will be the last ones to go out of shape, and the first ones to drop back in after a rainstorm), steelhead will be found in the same areas as in the larger rivers under the same conditions: next to the bank in the slower, less silty water.

In summary, there are two things to keep in mind when decoding small water: recognizing steelhead holding pockets and learning run timing. Beginners take note, learning on small streams will better prepare you to master larger water.

3.) Exceptions To The Norm: Tidewater and Canyons

These two areas are the most underfished portions of a steelhead river. Yet 95% of all rivers with runs of steelhead have either tidewater in the lower section or a canyon area somewhere along their length. Why aren't these areas visited by more anglers? Speculation says that a general lack of knowledge on how to fish these areas explains why they are so lonely. The truth is, even though most of the steelheaders work only the sections that have classic drifts with few variables, some of the best fishing to be had, winter and summer, can be found in the tidal and canyon stretches of rivers.

First let's look at tidewater. Fishing the tidal zones for steelhead can be a hit and miss affair. Success depends on how you read the water during the stages of the tide. An ideal time to fish tidal sections of rivers is during winter in the middle of a dry period with cold weather. When water conditions in the upper river are low, clear and cold, (33 to 38 degrees) saltwater will be around 45 degrees. This warmer water holds fish in the tidal portions until rains warm and increase the flow of the river.

One thing is certain when fishing tidewater. Steelhead are at their physical prime; they are the brightest and fight the hardest. When fishing changing tides, steelhead will move, and when steelhead move to a new position they are the most aggressive. Not only will you be lonely fishing tidewater, but you will be tangling with the fish at their best. Pick a river and locate the "head" of the tide. This is the area where there is no longer any saltwater influence, or the farthest point upstream where high tide no longer pushes freshwater backwards. Find the first pool or riffle that has a flat holding area at the head of the tide. This is the area you want to concentrate on. To understand steelhead behavior in the tidal sections (the key to hooking them with drift gear) we have to look at the river during three tidal stages: outgoing and low slack, incoming, and high slack.

Outgoing and low slack are the best times to be on tidal sections of rivers. This is because steelhead tend to pile up at the head of the tide, basically being pushed back downstream by the retreating water. During these outgoing conditions, water flows fairly strong with the current towards saltwater. You can fish the same way you would in the upper river, where the fish will be depends on water volume. If the river is flowing high and strong,

they will be on the edges, or the parting lines of the current, where there is the least amount of flow. If the water is low, look for them in the upper portion of the holding water where there is the most flow. During outgoing or low slack tides, reading the water is relevant to finding steelhead in the upper river.

During the incoming tide, however, things change. The few fishermen that fish the tidal portions of rivers do so only on the outgoing or low tides, because the fish are fairly easy to find. The misconception is that once the tide starts to come in, flooding the holding water, all the fish move up or have scattered, making fishing these portions of the tide senseless. Not so. What is actually happening is that the incoming tide has pushed the flowing piece of holding water backwards and has made the current edges, parting lines and riffles virtually disappear. In reality, the steelhead will not be scattered, but they will move. When the water starts to rise from the incoming tide, the fish will hold on the edges of the shoreline or estuary regardless of the present water height and clarity of the river. This may seem a bit weird, but don't look for the fish in the deepest portion of the "hole" when the tide is incoming. They won't be there. Steelhead in these conditions will hold in shallower water, from 3 to 6 feet, as long as there is cover. The temptation, especially in low water conditions, is to fish the part of the holding water with the most flow. The steelhead will be holding next to the sides of the incoming flow, out of the main current, even if it is minimal from the push of saltwater backing up the river. There are exceptions, however. They will

Canyon water can be the most difficult to access and fish, but can also be the most rewarding to the angler willing to hike.

move to the edges, yes, after the tide has been backing up the water for a half hour or so. Before that, steelhead will hold their position for a short period in the main portion of the holding water.

High slack is the toughest portion of the tide to fish, because you really have to work the water. At high slack, the fish tend to scatter and can be just about anywhere. The one constant at high slack is that most of the fish will still be toward the edges. The minimal amount of flow due to the water being backed up, especially at low flows or on small rivers, can make drift fishing all but impossible. Try getting a drift with a float, or switch to lures. The trick at high slack is to fish everything. Any piece of water in the tidal area that looks like it could meet the requirement to hide a steelhead, just may.

Canyons are a different enigma altogether. Typically, there is very little, or nothing, that resembles conventional steelhead holding water in canyon stretches. Steep, high rock walls and cliffs are the norm. In canyons, rivers are squeezed through a narrows, which in turn creates swift chutes, waterfalls and up-boils with varying currents. Add these characteristics to holes that may be 20 or more feet deep, and you have challenging conditions. These exotic fishing conditions are also difficult for steelhead to move through. Therefore, fish will rest in canyon holes and tend to stack there.

The major obstacle when fishing canyon water is access. Hiking in steep terrain is difficult, at times can be dangerous and should be attempted only by anglers in good physical condition. Canyon water is well worth the effort if you can reach it. Once

Many stretches of canyon water can be fished only during periods of low water. Stealth is a priority when canyon steelheading.

you get there, how do you read the water and find steelhead? For all the complexities of canyon holding water, there are only a few basic ground rules to follow to consistently hook fish.

The time to concentrate on canyons is during periods of low water, winter or summer, for two reasons: First, less flow makes it difficult for steelhead to negotiate chutes, roaring rapids and short falls. They will wait in the holes for more water before continuing upstream. These natural obstructions turn canyon holes into an almost sure thing during the run. Canyon pools are also some of the deepest portions of the river, which attract steelhead during low water periods of winter and summer. During winter's cold, deeper water will be a degree or two warmer. In summer, when other portions of the river may be running too warm, the canyon pools will be several degrees cooler due to sunlight being on the water for much shorter periods, and provide a higher degree of dissolved oxygen as a result of the falls and chutes. Secondly, the reduced flows tone down the cross-currents, up-boils and chutes that make fishing the canyons almost impossible during higher conditions. Even water height that may be ideal for other normal sections of the river with classic riffle-pool-tailout makeup will more often than not have too much volume for practical drift fishing.

Canyons are, however, fishable during classic and higher water conditions and should not be totally ignored. What typically happens to the holding water during these periods is that the amount of fishable water decreases dramatically. Remember, canyon water is defined by roaring rapids, waterfalls and chutes. This water runs much harder and swifter than in any other portion of the river. What you, the canyon angler, must do is find pieces of holding water that do not "blow out" during anything but moderate to low water conditions. These shorter sections of holding water created by increased flows can produce great action; steelhead will group there because it may be the only spot slow enough for them to rest. But beware, these short sections are normally at the very tail end of the pool, and most canyon holes do not provide the angler the luxury of giving chase to a steelhead. There is not as much room to control a hot fish, nor is it as easy to hold them in the fast water as it would be in lower water conditions.

While nearly all portions of canyon runs and pools may hold fish, the nature of the water—up-boils, cross-currents and unusual depth—dictates that the angler must search out portions of the canyon holding water that are receptive to traditional drift fishing techniques. The majority of the time steelhead will hold in the previously mentioned areas, rather than near the bottom of the river where you would expect them to be. If the holding water in the canyon has unusual depth (20 or more feet) the fish will often stratify, or lay suspended, anywhere from 3 to 15 feet down in the hole. Rarely will you find a steelhead in water deeper than 15 feet. This leaves one specific portion of the canyon pool to target, and that is the tailout.

A canyon pool "tailout" as defined here is any portion of the holding water that is shallow and slow enough to comfortably hold fish. Tailouts will be that area where the pool no longer has great depth (15 feet or less); cross-currents and up-boils give way to smoother, even current until the holding water either shallows up (rare in canyon holes) or more likely flows over a break and forms a new chute, rapid or falls. A canyon pool tailout can be just a few feet to over 100 feet long.

Again, even here in the canyons, read the water. Find the flat spots, the proper bottom makeup, the correct depth and you will find steelhead.

CHAPTER 3

TERMINAL GEAR AND RIGGING

Spend a day on one of the more popular rivers during a peak steelhead run. You'll discover there are as many different ways to rig terminal gear as there are fishermen. Everyone has their favorite arrangement of hook/drift bobber/leader/weight. It's no wonder there are so many ways to rig up. Go into one of the larger sporting goods outlets anywhere in steelhead country and check out the selections for the drift fisherman to choose from. Rows and rows of literally hundreds of colors, sizes and styles of drift bobbers; dozens of hook styles and sizes (even colors!); half a dozen premium monofilaments for leaders; and the same for incorporating lead weight to get it all down.

Despite all the differences in size, color, style, types/colors of line for leaders, and all the variations of weights—just about all of them will catch fish. However, choosing the right terminal outfit for current river conditions greatly increases your chance for a hookup.

Here in Chapter Three, we will be breaking down and discussing terminal rigging for drift fishing. We will look at drift bobbers—styles, sizes, what they are made of, why the addition of one is important to the drift fisherman, what they represent or imitate, plus commercially available bobbers and a few home-made styles that are very effective for hooking steelhead. We will also look at hooks—styles, practical sizes, designs to look for, how to match them with the proper sized drift bobber and how to make them and keep them sharp to effectively hold steelhead. The ever so important ties that bind—monofilament knots—will be explained and clearly shown.

Getting the terminal gear to the bottom, the weighting system, will be discussed, as pencil style and other forms of lead are compared to the slinky. We will compare the two weighting styles and show how, when and why one will out-perform the other in different holding water situations. We will match terminal outfits for all possible river conditions, covering height, clarity and temperature as they apply to all of the above. Finally, we will look at terminal outfits that were borrowed from other steelheading techniques: flies, plugs and thin-bladed spoons.

1.) Drift Bobbers

What is a "drift bobber", and where did it originate? Drift bobbers are an integral part of steelhead drift fishing. Trying to cope with changing water conditions without them would be difficult. So popular are drift bobbers today, it is rare to find a tackle box or vest without several dozen assorted sizes and styles. But steelheaders did not always have the advantages that drift bobbers provide. We do know that drift bobbers originally were used in Puget Sound and Olympic Peninsula steelhead rivers.

Cherry Bobber

The original drift bobber. This "cherry bobber," invented by Seattle barber Willis Korf, was the first artificial drift lure for steelhead.

Before 1952, when a barber from Seattle named Willis Korf let loose his innovative Cherry Bobber, such a thing did not exist. Previously, only three techniques were available to the steelheader: fly fishing, spoon fishing and drifting salmon roe. Mr. Korf wanted an inexpensive, fish catching lure that could be used in most or all river conditions. The cork-bodied, fluorescent red/orange Cherry Bobbers caught steelhead like crazy; for years they were the rage on Puget Sound rivers like the Skykomish and Puyallup. Korf's first drift bobbers were widely copied and lead to many offsprings; several of these designs and styles are still favorites today.

Ray Bobbers

Shaped like a child's spinning top, "Ray bobbers" like these (note the well-worn finish) were developed on Washington's Olympic Peninsula for steelhead that preferred a large profile drift lure.

The year 1953 saw the birth of the Ray Bobber and the Hoh Bug near the tiny lumber town of Forks. The Ray Bobber, popularized on the Bogachiel River, was a hollow, plastic drift bobber shaped like a child's toy spinning top. The name "Ray" probably came from the inventor. This large bobber (up to three inches long!) was a favorite of Olympic Peninsula steelheaders, as ocean-fresh fish preferred a larger profile drift lure than their inland counterparts. The Hoh Bug was originally made from the roots of cottonwood trees that grew near the Hoh River's banks. The roots were a dull yellow with green spots and, when hand-carved into drift bobbers, were found to attract steelhead from the same river. In 1954 the Sammy Special appeared. This was a smaller version of Korf's Cherry Bobber used on the Samish River near the town of Bellingham, hence the name. After the Sammy came the three most popular drift lures of all time: the Spin-N-Glo in 1954, the

Drift bobbers are the drift fisherman's universal tool. They can be matched in size, style and color to any river condition. The fish on the left hit a large, glow-in-the-dark spinning bobber in twelve inches of visibility, and the steelhead on the right picked up a tiny, round, subtle metallic blue bobber in gin-clear conditions.

Okie Drifter in 1956 and the Korky (now spelled Corkie) in 1963. These drift bobbers revolutionized steelhead drift fishing.

As the name "bobber" implies, it floats, but it is not the kind of bobber your mind conjures up, the old red and white plastic float used for panfishing, but the concept is the same. A drift bobber's main function is to keep the hook/bait at a greater than neutral buoyancy, just above the rocks and gravel, while traveling downstream with the current. A bobber's physical makeup is generally a high floating substance, such as cork, expanded polystyrene, hollow plastic or closed-cell foam. All commercially manufactured drift bobbers feature a hole through the center of the body that allows the bobber to slide freely onto the leader. When made commercially, these are coated with a thin plastic and/or painted. The drift bobber's position on the terminal gear never changes; they are always placed just above the hook(s), either resting on the eye of the hook or on a round bead. The bobber can be a multitude of shapes, all of them more or less round, varying to oval, cylindrical or triangular in profile. Some have beveled ends and/or wings, which give them more action than a plain, round style. These modifications to the body of the drift bobber make it wobble and/or spin in the current, giving them additional fish attracting qualities.

What does the drift bobber mimic? Since steelhead do not talk, we can only speculate. The general theory is that its roundish shape and size mimic salmon or steelhead roe on the loose, bouncing downstream. A better theory might be that because steelhead are territorial, they will try and remove any foreign object that happens into their holding water. Perhaps a latent feeding stimulus is triggered in the big sea-run rainbow when it comes back into fresh water, and while a steelhead will not actively seek out food, the colorful little bobbers coming by may be mistaken for food. Regardless of what a steelhead thinks a drift bobber represents, anglers know steelhead will take them, and that alone is reason enough.

The drift bobber has three main functions, and all attest to the bobber's unique usefulness in steelhead drift fishing. One, by suspending the hook/bait just above the bottom, hooks are kept sharper. Bait will stay on for longer periods, as frequent contact with rocks will dull hooks and pound off delicate baits like roe and sand shrimp in short order. Two, the steelheader can match sizes, styles and colors of drift bobber to current water conditions. For example, the addition of a large, highly visible spinning drift bobber to a bait will increase the chance a fish will see

it in cloudy, limited visibility water conditions. By toning down or increasing size/color, the bobber is the universal tool to the drift fisherman in any water level and color. Three, the most important function of a drift bobber derives from its buoyancy, your offering will be presented where a steelhead can see it. Anadromous fish like steelhead and salmon cannot look down unless they turn their bodies sideways. At rest, their cone of vision is only straight ahead or up. By presenting your bait with a buoyant drift bobber (or the bobber alone) at the eye-level of the steelhead, you have greatly increased the chances for a hookup.

How a steelhead reacts to a drift bobber depends on the style of bobber but also water temperature. More or less round drift bobbers (such as a Corkie) impart very little action when drifted against the current; and this seems to agitate fish less than a spinning or wobbling bobber such as the Birdie, Spin-N-Glo, or Cheater. The take on a round bobber will be a subtle stop, or slight pull, especially in cold water (33 to 42 degrees) or limited visibility conditions. When the water is warmer, (43 to 60 degrees) you can expect more aggressive takes, especially on bobbers with wobbling or spinning action.

How is a drift bobber used? As stated earlier, all drift bobbers have a hole through the center of their bodies, just wide enough for monofilament line to pass through. All non-spinning drift bobbers should simply be slid onto the leader and allowed to rest just above the eye of the hook. You may want to slip a small (3 to 5mm) plastic bead between the hook eye and the drift bobber. Other than perhaps adding a bit more color and profile to the bobber, the bead does create a larger bite area between the hook point and the widest spot on the bobber.

There is no need to affix the drift bobber next to the hook by jamming a toothpick or twig into the hole to keep it in position. Since a drift bobber always travels downstream ahead of the weighting system (lead,etc.), there will always be current forcing the bobber down against the hook, keeping it from riding up on the leader. The only time a drift bobber will slip up the leader away from the hook is if you are working dead slow water or a back-eddy. In these two situations, you want to abandon the drift bobber and change techniques. (See Chapter Four: Float Fishing.)

Spinning drift bobbers are also slid directly onto the leader without being fixed against the hook. While the use of a bead is optional with a round-style bobber, a bead is mandatory with a rotating one. On a spinning drift bobber (such as a Spin-N-Glo or

Birdie) the bead acts as a bearing, allowing the bobber to spin freely. This bead bearing not only lets the bobber spin faster and easier, it prevents line twist that would be caused by the bobber pushing down onto the hook eye while revolving in the current. One tip: When putting on a new spinning drift bobber, take note of the bottom of the bobber at the hole. More often than not, the coloring or dipping process has made a rough point or edge near the hole. This uneven bottom will affect the action of the bobber, not allowing it to spin with ease. Take a nail file and smooth the bottom flush with the hole. This will ensure a free-spinning bobber.

Out of the several styles of spinning drift bobbers available on the market, only the Spin-N-Glo has a special feature, one that the manufacturer may not even be aware of. When purchasing Spin-N-Glo's, look down on the top of the bobber. In some cases the hole is not quite lined up directly in the center of the lure but is slightly off-center. These are the ones to buy. Along with their spinning action, these off-center Spin-N-Glo's will wobble rapidly in the current, giving them an added bit of attraction to steelhead, definitely something to remember when fishing in cold water conditions (33 to 42 degrees). The added action helps "wake up" lethargic steelhead.

In the case of round drift bobbers, there is no top or bottom; either side can be facing up, it makes no difference. With bobbers that are non-symmetrical, there is definitely a top and bottom to them, and how they sit on top of the hook affects their action and hooking ability. The rotating drift bobbers are designed to sit above the hook a certain way. Oval shaped spinning bobbers like the Birdie have tapered wings the length of their bodies; one end of the wings is wider than the opposite end. Set on top of the bead with the thin end facing up, they will spin faster and easier than if the fat end of the wings are facing up. This requires a careful inspection before sliding the bobber onto the leader, as with these styles the ends are not easily told apart without a closer look. In triangle or diamond-shaped spinning drift bobbers, it is easy to tell the top from bottom. The narrow end always sits on top of the bead, and the "top" will always be where the wings are attached to the body. The Spinning Cheater and the Spin-N-Glo are the best examples.

Other non-symmetrical drift bobbers also have a top and bottom. The Okie and the Cheater are good examples. There are two important reasons to position them with the narrow end toward the hook. One, the current's pressing against the fat end of the bobber will impart action to the lure, making it wobble and dance, adding another steelhead attracting quality. Two, the fat end's being positioned down towards the eye of the hook tends to kill the action and shrink the gap between bobber and hook. Too small a gap causes missed strikes.

This leads us to the most important question: How large a drift bobber should you use? The answer lies in current water conditions. The style, size and color of bobber should match water temperature, water color and in some instances, water speed. (This will be discussed in more detail later in this chapter.) However, there is one rule of thumb that *never* varies. Before casting, you have to match the size drift bobber to the size hook you are using. This is done by setting the bobber between the barb and the shank on the inside of the hook bend. If the bobber passes between the barb and shank, barely touches while being passed through, or is a hair larger than the gap, it is the correct size. You want a gap between the point of the hook and the outside of the drift bobber that does not block access to the bite area. (See photo for proper drift bobber—hook match.)

Hook/Bobber Match

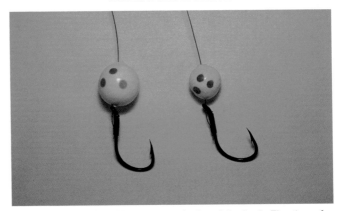

The size of the drift bobber must match size of the hook. The circumference of the large bobber on the left extends past the tine of the hook, interfering with the "bite" area. The bobber on the right is smaller, and does not block the hook point.

Drift bobber sizes relate directly to whether bait is used or not. Normally, if the bobber is used in tandem with bait, the drift bobber is smaller than it would be if fished solo. With bait, a large profile bobber is not necessary; the bait itself takes care of that. The bobber's main function with bait is to give it buoyancy and a dab of color. Without bait, the bobber is the only attractant and must therefore be somewhat larger.

From the time Willis Korf changed steelhead drift fishing in the 1950s' to today, we steelheaders have more sizes, styles and colors of commercially made drift bobbers than a person could use in a lifetime. Here is a list of commercially made drift bobbers and manufacturers, as well as a description of basic function.

Yakima Bait Company
(Corkies, Spin-N-Glo's, Wobble-Glo's)
P.O. Box 310
Granger, Washington 98392
(509)-854-1311

Corkies

The Corkie is, without a doubt, the most popular drift bobber of all time. As its name implies, it was originally a cork bodied lure, but now all Corkies are made from high-floating polystyrene. The Corkie is available in six different sizes: #14 (smallest), #12, #10, #8, #6 and #4 (largest). Sizes #14 through #8 are the most practical and popular; the larger sizes (#6 and #4) are used primarily for large river salmon. Corkies are available in natural, fluorescent glow and metallic colors/finishes. Its simple round design does not impart any extra action to the bobber. The three main functions of Corkies are: (1) to add buoyancy to natural bait, (2) as an added bit of color and profile to bait, and (3) used alone or with flourescent yarn as an attractor. Steelhead tend to stop the Corkie on a pickup, the same take normally experienced with bait. The Corkie is probably fished alone as much as it is used with bait.

Spin-N-Glo's

The Spin-N-Glo is a long triangular-shaped drift bobber fitted with a pair of wings to impart a spinning action when drifted with river currents. It was originally made with a cork body, and as of this writing, still is. The Spin-N-Glo is available in 8 sizes, from #14 (smallest), #12, #10, #8, #6, #4, #2 and #0 (largest). Sizes #14 through #6 are primarily used by steelhead drift fishermen, the larger sizes (#4 through #0) are normally employed by plunkers in high water or for river salmon. They are available in natural, fluorescent glow and metallic colors/finishes. The Spin-N-Glo has three functions to the drift fisherman: (1) to be used solo or with bait when plunking or drifting in high water conditions, (2) to be used in tandem with bait to add buoyancy and profile, and (3) as an attractor, either solo or with yarn or bait. Two types of wings are available with the Spin-N-Glo: the standard white flexible rubber and stiff, reflective mylar (the latter spins much faster due to the non-flexibility of the wings). The mylar winged bobber works best in slow water, while the rubber winged traditional performs best in swifter currents. The Spin-N-Glo is an excellent choice for exciting large steelhead in cold water. Besides offering visual attraction, the spinning action of the bobber creates a vibration that makes it the most effective style in cloudy, off-colored water. The Spin-N-Glo should always be fished with a bead between the bobber and the hook eye, allowing the bobber to spin freely with the greatest action possible, and to avoid line twist.

Wobble-Glo's

The Wobble-Glo is an oval-shaped, cork bodied drift bobber that first made its appearance back in 1957. It is available in five sizes: #12 (smallest), #10, #8, #6 and # 4 (largest). Not as popular as the Corkie or the Spin-N-Glo, the Wobble-Glo is an effective bobber for basically the same reasons as the Spin-N-Glo: unusual action is imparted to it when drawn against the current. The front

of the bobber is flat and angled at 45 degrees. This gives the Wobble-Glo a lip, much like a diving plug, and results in much the same kind of action. As with any moving lure, the Wobble-Glo's plug-like wiggle more often than not will draw violent takes from steelhead. The Wobble-Glo is primarily fished solo as an attractor, much the same as a plug or spoon, but can be used in tandem with bait.

Luhr Jensen and Sons
(Okie Drifters, Birdies, Sammy Specials, Cherry Bobbers)
P.O. Box 297
Hood River, Oregon 97031
1-800-535-1711

Okies

The Okie, along with the Corkie, is one of the most popular drift bobbers. Originally made from a shell of hollow plastic and painted, today's Okies are made of high-floating styrene and are available in natural and fluorescent colors. Although the plastic ones (in this fisherman's eyes) were more durable and had a superior finish (color) and profile than the new ones, they are still the author's favorite all-time drift bobber. Okies are available in four sizes: #1 (smallest), #2, #3 and #4 (largest). The Okie is a diamond shaped drift bobber with a defined wide top and tapered bottom. The Okie, made to imitate a cluster of roe, imparts a rapid wobble when pulled against the current. Its main functions as a drift lure are: (1) it adds buoyancy to bait, (2) it is fished solo as an egg imitation or with yarn, and (3) it is used in tandem with bait as added color and profile. The Okie, along with the Corkie and Cheater, are the best styles of drift bobbers to fish solo.

Birdies

The Birdie is a flat/oval-shaped, styrene-bodied spinning drift bobber. It is available in natural and fluorescent colors. The Birdie, has wings that run the length of its body, and unlike other styles of spinning drift bobbers (such as the Spin-N-Glo), the wings are a part of the body of the lure, not an addition. The Birdie can be fished two different ways, depending on which way the bobber is placed on top of the hook. Close examination of the Birdie shows the wings are fat on one end and tapered to thin on the other. When the thin part of the wings ride up (facing away from the hook), the Birdie will spin rapidly in the current. This is an advantage in slower currents. When the bobber is reversed, with the fat end of the wings facing up, the Birdie will spin more slowly, an advantage in swifter currents. The Birdie is available in four sizes: #0 (smallest), #1, #3 and #5 (largest). The main functions of the Birdie are: (1) fished solo as an attractor lure or with yarn, (2) as added buoyancy to bait, and (3) to add color and profile to bait.

Sammy Specials

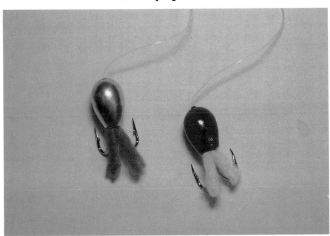

The Sammy Special is an oddity among commercially made drift bobbers, it comes pre-rigged with leader and hooks. The Sammy has not a single, but a double, nickel-plated hook, along with dual strands of fluorescent colored yarn coming out of the bottom of its balsa wood body. The Sammy is drifted solo as an attractor, as there is no practical way to use it in tandem with bait due to the lack of a bait loop on the drift bobber. The Sammy Special is available in natural and fluorescent colors, and two

sizes: #3 (smallest), and #5 (largest). The Sammy is a high-floating drift bobber and performs best in moderate to high water conditions.

Cherry Bobbers

The Cherry Bobber is manufactured by Luhr Jensen almost identically to Willis Korf's original many decades ago. This old-timer still attracts steelhead. The Cherry Bobber is fished solo as an attractor lure, either drifted or plunked. The Cherry Bobber is unusual, as it is the only drift bobber ever manufactured with a spinner blade set on top of the body of the bobber. The Cherry Bobber comes in only one color, just like the original: fire red/fluorescent. The spinner blades come in four colors/finishes: hammered nickel; hammered brass; fire orange/silver plate; and nickel/silver plate. All come with a wire shaft through the center of the body and a treble hook on the end of the wire shaft. The Cherry Bobber is available in five sizes: #1 (smallest), #2, #3, #4 and #5 (largest).

Beau Mac Enterprises
(Cheaters, Flashing And Spinning Cheaters, The Pill)
1802 37th Way S.E.
Auburn, Washington 98002
(206)-939-8607

Cheaters

The Cheater is an oval, expanded polystyrene bodied drift bobber, with one end of the bobber wider. In shape, it closely resembles the old Ray Bobber. First produced in 1986, Cheaters have rapidly become one of the most popular and effective commercially available drift bobbers. They are available in 70 natural, fluorescent and metallic colors/finishes. The Cheater is normally fished with the narrower end down, on top of the hook eye. When fished solo, the Cheater will do a tight, slow wobble when drifted against the current. The main functions of a Cheater are: (1) fished solo or with fluorescent yarn as an attractor, (2) added buoyancy when used in tandem with bait, and (3) as an added bit of color with bait. The Cheater is available in seven sizes: #14 (smallest), #12, #10, #8, #6, #4 and #2 (largest).

Flashing and Spinning Cheaters

The Flash and Spin Cheater is simply a Cheater fixed with mylar wings and was the first drift bobber to be fitted with them. It is available in six sizes: #10 (smallest), #8, #6, #4, #2 and #2/0 Magnum (largest). The Flash and Spin Cheater comes in natural, fluorescent, and metallic finishes, as well as eleven different colored wings. Its mylar wings make it spin very fast; this feature makes it a good choice in slow, cold or off-colored water. The main functions of a Flash and Spin Cheater are: (1) fished solo or with flourescent yarn as an attractor lure, (2) as added buoyancy in tandem with bait, and (3) as an added color attractor and increased profile with bait. A spinning drift bobber like the Flashing and Spinning Cheater should be used with a bead between bobber and hook to avoid line twist and to allow the spinning bobber maximum action.

Pills

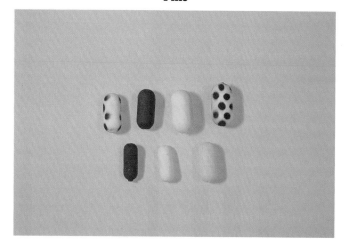

The Pill is shaped exactly as it sounds, in the same proportions as a Tylenol capsule. This expanded polystyrene bobber does not impart any added action when drifted against current, but its slender profile and almost total lack of water resistance make it a choice of drift fishermen in swift conditions, or when used in tandem with long baits like worms or sand shrimp. The Pill is available in natural and fluorescent finishes, and in three sizes: #1 (smallest), #2 and #3 (largest). The Pill is used: (1) in tandem with bait to add buoyancy, and (2) as an attractor for added color and enlarged profile with bait.

2.) Home-made Drift Bobbers

A fly-fishing friend of mine tells me there is a great deal of satisfaction that comes from catching a steelhead on a fly you have tied yourself. The same satisfaction comes from hooking a fish on a hand-made lure. Home-made drift bobbers are not only fun to make, they are inexpensive. Best of all they will sometimes outfish anything you can get commercially. The important thing is that they work, and deserve mention. There are two specific styles of home-made drift bobbers available to the imaginative steelheader.

Rags

The "rag," properly rigged.

This contraption is the most bizarre looking device you will ever come across on a steelhead river. Known by many names— "rag," "bomb," "slob," or "sloth," just to pick out a few of the most popular, this drift bobber does one thing well and that is draw strikes from steelhead.

The design of the rag varies little. The two major components of this bobber are strands of fluorescent yarn and a small cylinder of soft, closed-cell foam. This foam is more commonly known as "backer rod." It is used in the construction industry for insulation when installing new windows in homes. This backer foam is normally available in 1/2 and 3/4 inch diameter. To build a rag, cut off a piece of backer foam from 3/4 to an 1-1/4 inches long. With the aid of a large sewing needle, thread a 4 inch piece of yarn (not too thick or it won't go through the eye of the needle) halfway into the eye of the needle. Insert different colors of yarn through the top half of the foam cylinder until the yarn hangs out approximately 3/4 to 1 inch on each side. The yarn should be hanging out of the foam at all the same length. You can weave one to six different colors of yarn through the lure. The only color pattern limits are your imagination.

After all the desired colors of yarn have been woven through and trimmed evenly, add the hook and leader. Before threading the line into the foam, slide on a 5mm red bead so it lies on top of the eye of the hook. Take the same sewing needle and thread the end of the leader through the eye. Center the needle at the bottom of the foam cylinder (the end without the yarn) and push straight through to the top, weaving the line through the center of the rag until it slides down snug on top of the bead. The bead keeps the foam from digging into the hook eye. You can adjust the diameter, length and number/brightness of yarn colors to water conditions. Rags are inexpensive to make; as of this writing you can get a 100 feet of backer rod at a glass/window outlet for less than 5 dollars.

The home-made rag has one feature that commercially made drift bobbers do not: it floats higher in the drift than any other bobber. Due to the rather large body of closed-cell foam, the rag will ride about 4 to 6 inches higher in the drift than all other drift bobbers. This is a great feature when fishing in faster water, where water force will push a floating drift bobber down against the rocks; or in rivers with large boulder bottoms, the high floater will be seen more readily. Remember, steelhead cannot see down, only straight out and upwards. A high floating drift bobber like the rag always stays in the fish's cone of vision. Because of the rag's soft foam body, steelhead tend to chew on this drift bobber longer than a hard bodied one. The rag's closed cell, foam body accepts scents well, especially when they are injected into the center of the lure. When a fish takes the rag, it is rarely a soft mouthing; even in cold or limited visibility conditions, a hard swipe from an enraged fish is the norm.

The rag is an exceptional drift bobber in river conditions with some color. This 16 lb. February native gave our boat a tour of the lower Hoh River.

Theories as to the origin of the rag vary. Seattle outdoor writer John Beath claims it started on the Skagit; twenty-year Olympic Peninsula guide John Riedesel first saw the rag on the Satsop; but the earliest tales of the rag come from the Peninsula, specifically the Humptulips River, near the town of Hoquiam. Joe Butorac, long-time Peninsula steelhead guide, tells this story: "The Humptulips River was the favorite steelhead hot-spot in western Washington back in 1962, when I first saw the rag. The Humptulips was the last river in the state to have a three-steelhead limit. That should tell you how good the fishing was. All the local guides worked "The Hump" back then, and we were always looking for some new technique that would keep us on top of the fish.

"One week in January, there was a group of guys from (the town of) Olympia really getting into fish. They were out-fishing everyone—including us guides who really knew the river—by five to one. When we all demanded to know what they were using, they produced this white foam thing with yarn hanging out of it. They said it was something they had put together out of materials at the job site (they were in the construction field), and had no idea it would work so well."

If you cannot find the components or want to buy a rag already put together, the Trophy Tackle Company of Bellevue, Washington, (1-206-435-8624) markets pre-made rags. They can also be found in some major Northwest tackle shops.

Sponges

Sponges, properly rigged.

No fancy names for this one, it is just that, a chunk of sponge. Since sponges feature closed air cells and are soft after soaking in water, they make a natural-feeling home-made drift bobber. A plain, synthetic household sponge, the kind that sits next to the kitchen sink, works best. All you need to do is to get a pair of scissors and cut the sponge into small round balls. Wetting the sponge first makes it pliable and easier to work with.

Thread the line (leader) through the center of the sponge ball, using the same sewing needle you used to thread the rag. A bead may also be added onto the leader on top of the eye of the hook before the sponge is threaded on. The sponge drift bobber may be fished alone, or like the rag, you can thread different colored strands of yarn through the center for added attraction. Make the sizes and colors of sponges to match water conditions.

The sponge has one drawback. The water must be squeezed out after every few casts to retain buoyancy. It is a sponge, after all. The sponge does give the drift fisherman a natural feeling, soft lure that won't be immediately rejected by a steelhead, and its soft body will not inhibit the bite area of the hook like a hard-bodied drift bobber. The sponge also holds scents very well, better than any other drift bobber, commercial or home-made.

Artificial Soft Plastic Baits

Soft plastic artificial baits, while they do not work nearly as well as their real counterparts, do get the attention of steelhead. All commercially available, soft plastic baits mimic salmon/steelhead roe to a degree, some more closely than others. Steelhead tend to chew on these soft baits for a split second longer than hard drift bobbers, and that trait makes artificials very popular in areas that do not allow natural baits for steelhead fishing. Soft

An assortment of soft plastic baits, all properly rigged, from left: Egg Bumpers, Steelhead Candy, a Gooey Bob and a Crazy Egg.

plastic baits neither float nor sink, but rather have a neutral buoyancy. These baits are often manufactured with a scent in the plastic to make them more attractive.

Here are some of the most popular and successful soft plastic baits used on steelhead rivers.

Gooey Bob (Luhr Jensen)

The Gooey Bob is the close kin of the Okie Drifter, except for its soft texture. The Gooey Bob resembles a tight cluster of immature roe. It is manufactured with a small diameter, clear plastic tube through the center of the lure to allow for a leader to slip through. The Gooey Bob is fished two ways: either set on the top of the hook like a drift bobber, or a hook can be worked through the plastic tube and then set on the bottom/shank of the hook. The Gooey Bob is undoubtedly the most popular commercially made soft plastic bait. It has a tremendous following on British Columbia steelhead rivers. It is available in three sizes and several natural colors, light pink and orange being most popular.

Egg Bumpers, (Capitol Tackle)
Steelhead Candy, (Beau Mac Enterprises) and
Super Spawn (Super Spawn, P.O. Box 738, Noblesville, Indiana 46060 (317) 773-4009.)

Egg Bumpers, Steelhead Candy, and Super Spawn are soft plastic mini-clusters of artificial roe. Each is made up of a cluster of 3 or 4 plastic, mature-sized eggs connected by a thin nylon string or plastic. These can be snipped off to fish them as single clusters, or as 2 and 3, depending on water conditions and the whims of the angler. The most common way to fish them is to use 2 of the small clusters together, setting them in an egg loop on top of the hook, letting both small clusters hang off each side. They are often fished with a drift bobber, solo with yarn, or solo under a float.

Crazy Egg
Worth Company
P.O. Box 88
Stevens Point, Wisconsin 54481

The Crazy Egg is an oddity. What it resembles is a single salmon egg with a curly tail. The Crazy Egg, unlike any other soft plastic lure, imparts action to the tail when drifted against the current. The tail wiggles rapidly, and is undoubtedly the

main attraction feature. Often used solo, the Crazy Egg is impaled through the round egg body and allowed to sit on the bend/shank of the hook with the tail facing away from the hook. It imitates a newly hatching egg that has drifted out of the redd. I am told this is an effective low, clear water drift lure but have little evidence to back it up.

Pink Worm

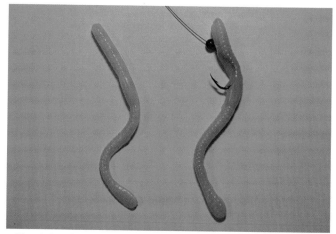

The pink, soft plastic worm (left), and the same properly rigged (right).

This distant cousin of the nightcrawler is possibly the most popular soft plastic lure in British Columbia. I do know that during several steelheading trips to the west side of Vancouver Island, I have seen the ground alive with light pink worms after heavy rains. Undoubtedly, a good number of these wash into the streams and the steelhead key on them. Simply a soft plastic, light pink replica of an earthworm, the pink worm is made locally and widely by at least half a dozen entrepreneurs and companies. (The most popular and widely distributed is The Steely Worm by Gibbs/Nortac Co., 7455 Conway Avenue, Burnaby, British Columbia, V5E-2PT) Four and a half to 6 inch worms are commonly fished solo beneath a float on a single hook fastened an inch or so below the head of the worm, while smaller 2 to 3-1/2 inch worms are threaded onto hooks below drift bobbers. The pink worm has a natural, seductive slow wiggle when drifted against the current. Curly-tailed versions give an alluring "swimming" action to the worm adding quite a bit of movement. The pink, soft plastic worm is especially effective in moderate to medium/high water that has a bit of color to it.

3.) Hooks

Hooks are the most important part of the drift fisherman's arsenal. The best presentation, the best bait, all the premium monofilaments and expensive state-of-the-art rods and reels won't be worth a wader leg full of cold water if you are not employing the proper hook.

When selecting hooks, ignore manufacturer's advertising claims about their products. Be a visual selector. The question is not which brand to choose, there are a half a dozen companies that manufacture quality hooks. Some are more expensive than others, and this is justified in strength and degree of sharpness. However, there are too many fishermen out there with different opinions. Every steelheader has a brand preference, and if you are

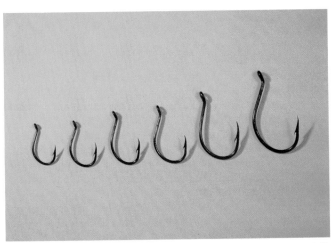

The six sizes of steelhead drift fishing hooks, from left: #4, #2, #1, #1/0, #2/0 and #3/0. Hooks similar in design to these will be the ones to use.

successful with that specific brand, far be it from me to suggest changing to another. You could argue the merits of one style of hook by one company for hours, and you will still find crowds of anglers that disagree with you. So, instead of picking out brand names, we will look objectively at what makes an effective steelhead hook, and what to look for when buying them.

Most hook companies have their hooks marked on the packaging that label them as "salmon/steelhead hooks," "salmon egg hooks," "steelhead hooks" or "octopus" style. These are the ones to look for. These styles all have up-turned eyes. The up-turned eye is the hook choice of the drift fisherman. The eye in this bent-

back position does not interfere with the transfer of power on the hook-set, does not shrink the bite area of the hook the way a down-turned eye would, allows you to easily tie an egg-loop knot (the most common knot for attaching leader to hook), and allows beads and drift bobbers to set on top of the hook so that they will not interfere with the bite area or impede their action, such as spinning. Choose hooks that have no bait, or snell barbs, on the hook shank. They are sometimes common on smaller sized steelhead-style hooks. If you cannot find a hook style without them, flatten them with pliers before tying on a leader. The sharp point on the bait barb will cut through monofilament.

These styles, regardless of brand, have a more or less rounded design. Rounded styles feature a relatively short shank, a half-circle round base and should come up from the bottom of the round base so the tip of the hook is at least half-way up the shank. Any hook with the business end not at least half again as long as the hook shank will have two strikes against it. One, larger and very active fighters will come loose with greater frequency due to the hook not having enough hold area. The longer the length from the bottom of the hook to the tip, the more "meat" (I hate to use that analogy, but it makes a point) it holds. Two, leverage on hookset will be lost to a degree with a shorter end. The leverage point on any hook is halfway up the shank. Power transferred from rod to hook is lost by degrees as the front of the hook is shorter.

Practical steelhead hooks come in six sizes: #4 (smallest), #2, #1, #1/0, #2/0 and #3/0 (largest). Any hook smaller than a #4 has minimal bite area in the gap, and even though they are a popular size with light-liners, the #4 is absolutely the smallest practical sized hook for holding a fish as large and powerful as a steelhead. The sizes of hooks that are the most common and practical

This steelhead was landed thanks to a sharp hook. The fish is hooked through the solid-bone mandible of the mouth. A hook not properly sharpened would not have penetrated and been rejected immediately.

are #1, #1/0 and #2/0. These fit into the widest range of use from low to high water and work the best in tandem with the most common sized drift bobbers. The #3/0 is the largest hook you should ever need in steelhead drift fishing. If there is a steelhead out there that can bend out a quality #3/0 hook, I would be pleasantly surprised to see such a behemoth. Any hook larger than a #3/0 could do serious damage to a steelhead, as larger hooks have a tendency to go a little deep, occasionally going through the fish's eyes or causing excessive bleeding. When practicing strictly catch and release, it is best to stick with the smallest size hook possible, so that little damage to the fish's mouth is done. Some river systems have a hook size restriction, so as always before you fish, please check the regulations.

Look for "flat spots" such as these, before the river begins to slope downward and the water enters the break.

The most important consideration in selecting a drift fishing hook is to check the design of the points. It is imperative that the brand of hook you choose has a long, straight tine (the part of the hook from the barb to the point). Compare different brands of hooks and you will see the difference. Some will have long, straight tines; some will be shorter and wider. Most of the short tined hooks have curved tines, these are not the ones to buy. Logically, a straight pointed hook is much easier to set than a curved one. Avoid the short, wide curved styles and brands. A long, straight tine is important because it can be set into the hard mouth of a steelhead (or salmon or any anadromous fish) with *half* the force of a short, curved, wide-tined hook. Think about it. What would take more force to push in, something thin or wide, straight or curved? Wide, short tined hooks will cause you to lose a lot of fish. What happens is the angler will set the hook with plenty of force, feel the fish twist once, twice and then come free. The short tined hook point, while it may have been razor sharp, was too wide for the amount of force needed to send it deep enough to hold. Besides being harder to set into the hard, bony plates of a steelhead's mouth, a short tined hook cannot be resharpened. The point is already short, any attempts at resharpening will only make the point shorter and that much harder to set. With a long, thin-tined hook, you will have the option of resharpening a dull hook, sometimes more than once without losing the thin, easy-setting feature. Repeat: choose a brand and style of hook that has a long, thin, straight tine.

Thickness of the hook is important. Your hook of choice should be of medium thickness. Avoid fine wire hooks in sizes #1 through #3/0. While fine wire is acceptable in the two smallest sizes (#4 and #2) to allow for an easier hookset with ultra-light rods and low pound test line, fine wire will not take the strain of heavier weighted rod blanks and heavier pound test lines. They will straighten much too easily. On the opposite end, avoid hooks that are "super-double-strong." These hooks are easy to spot; they look clumsy, and are much thicker than hooks of medium thickness. They are also somewhat impractical for steelheading. While they will certainly not bend out under the strain of a large fish, they will be difficult to set properly into the fish's mouth. This is the same reason we avoid short tined hooks: thick hooks will have a wide, short point. Plus, without exception they will be more expensive.

When you have chosen a style of hook that meets the criteria, take a look at the barb, if the style has one. (Many fishermen are using hooks that are manufactured barbless. These sans-a-barb hooks make it easy to hook and release steelhead, and do less damage to a fish's mouth than a barbed hook. I recommend this style over any with a barb.) Some hooks have well defined barbs with a wide flare; others are very small in comparison to the hook itself. Regardless of the size/shape/flare of the barb, you will solidly hook a greater percentage of steelhead if you pinch the barb down. For the same reason you would choose a long tined hook over a short, wide one, you will want to reduce the width of the barb. A wide, flared barb is undoubtedly the number one reason for lost fish. It takes a tremendous amount of transferred force to drive a hook into a steelhead's mouth, more than double that when adding a wide barb to the formula. If you insist on using a barb on the hook (you will not lose fish because of a lack of a barb, by simply keeping a tight line during the fight you will land as many as if the hook had a barb on it), take a pair of pliers and bend the barb half-way down. By doing this you have left yourself plenty of barb to hold a wildly fighting fish and lessened the force needed to set the hook past the barb by one half.

Hooks are available in an assortment of colors: red, green, blue, gold, nickel (silver), black and natural bronze finish. As far as one color having an advantage over another, or an advantage over plain bronze or black, nowhere have I seen evidence of this. If you are successful with a plain, natural finish, or one specific color under certain water conditions, by all means stick with it. Confidence in your gear will catch as many fish as anything else. What is known about colored hooks is that they are more expensive. Until someone, somewhere, can come up with solid evidence that one color will outfish a plain bronze or black finish, I will continue to save money by purchasing the non-colored ones.

Now that you can identify the right size and style (and perhaps color) of hook for drift fishing, the hooks must be kept sharp to perform their best. Only a very sharp hook will catch in a steelhead's mouth long enough to tell if it is indeed a fish on those soft mouthings; only a sharp hook will hold a fish after one of those "hit-and-run" strikes that give you no reaction time to set a hook; and only a razor-sharp hook allows for the easiest of hooksets. I have found just two brands of hooks that are sharp enough out of the box to be suitable for steelheading, and only one is a drift fishing hook. (The other is a hook used for flies.) I won't name them, but I will say that all other brands, regardless of manufacturer's claims, need to be sharpened before use. Even the two brands I won't name need to be sharpened on occasion. To produce the "ultra-sharp" hook point needed for easy hooksets, give the hook tine a three-edged sharpening. This is best done with a flat, diamond-surfaced sharpener. The fine flat surface, unlike most files, puts the smoothest, sharpest point on hooks. The flat, fine diamond file works best with smaller hooks from #4 to #1/0. A good quality, fine-grooved file should be your second choice, especially for larger hooks, #2/0 to #3/0. The three-edged point should be sharpened as it sounds, on both sides of the tine, and on the front of the point. By doing it this way, you have created four knife-like edges around the tine of the hook. These sharp edges help to cut through the tough mouth of a steelhead, allowing for an easier hookset.

Also, forget the old bad habit of scraping a hook point across the thumbnail to check for sharpness. By doing this, you are taking the extra sharpness away from your hook and dulling the point! Would you run your hook point over a rock after sharpening it? Certainly not! This is similar to what happens when a freshly sharpened hook point is rammed into a hard thumbnail. Check for proper sharpness by lightly touching the point with the tip of your finger. This will tell you immediately if it is sharp, and skin is a lot easier on a sharp point than a hard nail.

If you momentarily snag up, resulting in the tine of the hook being completely bent out of shape, cut off the hook and replace it. Attempting to bend the point back will weaken it. It will also cost you a fish. Hooks are relatively inexpensive, so take a few moments and retie a new leader.

3.) Knots

A drift fisherman should know several strong knots to hold—and land—a powerful steelhead. This spring fish tests this angler's knot-tying skills by tailwalking.

All steelheader's have favorite knots for monofilament line. And most anglers, myself included, use a minimum of knots to get them by while on the river. For all practical purposes, the steelheader only needs a few efficient, strong knots to fish effectively year around. This part of the chapter will concentrate on doing just that, showing the basic knots that benefit the drift fisherman.

Any knot in monofilament line creates a weak point, regardless of how strong that knot may be. Knowing this before you begin to tie a knot, make sure that each knot tied in the swivel or on the hook is done with patience and perfection. We all have, at one point or another on the river, cried the blues when a steelhead has broken off more easily than it should have for the pound test we were using. Take a second to examine the knot after you have tied it. Do all the wraps lay evenly and snugly next to each other? Overlaying wraps will cut each other and break. Gaps in the wraps will cause a burn in the mono when sudden pressure is applied, such as setting the hook. Burned line is weakened and breaks easily. Here is a very important tip when tying a knot. Just before pulling the knot snug tight, moisten the knot with a bit of saliva or river water. This will avoid monofilament burn from the friction of pulling the knot tight. Take your time, tie your knots so they are always perfect, and you will rarely have to agonize over a lost steelhead due to "a bad knot".

The most important knot that a drift fisherman must learn—and master—is the bumper knot, or egg loop knot. This is the most versatile, as well as strongest knot for attaching leader to hook. It has a slightly better than 90% line strength ratio. (Example: If the line would break at 10 pound test, the knot will break at 9 pounds.) This knot features even wraps of line down the hook shank, with the main leader coming out of the center of the wraps leading through the hook eye, creating a small loop. This loop on the hook may be opened (this is what holds bait snug to the hook) or where yarn is tied onto the line. (See diagram.)

Egg Loop

Start with about 24" Leader

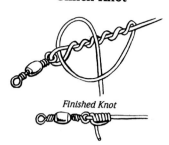

8 wraps

Continue original wrap (6 more)

Pull out slack

Finished Knot

A small amount of colored yarn may be tied onto loop. It is an easy way to open the loop, especially with cold fingers.

Finished Egg Loop with yarn and eggs.

The blood knot is not so easy to tie, but is a necessity to the steelhead drift fisherman. The blood knot, with an 85% strength rating joins two sections of monofilament; the closer in pound tests, the easier this knot is to tie. The blood knot takes some time to learn and is somewhat clumsy to tie, but it is the best line splicing knot available. (See diagram.)

Blood Knot

Finished Knot

The knots that are tied onto each end of the swivel connecting mainline to leader are the most frequently used on the river. These knots must be relatively easy to tie and must be strong. There are three specific connector knots a drift fisherman can use.

The first is the easiest and most common knot used by drift fishermen, the clinch knot. It has a 75% strength rating and is recommended whenever using a dropper to lead. This knot will break before any other on the terminal rigging. It is, however, simple and strong and can be tied with cold hands. (See diagram.)

Clinch Knot

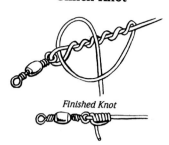

Finished Knot

The second knot is an improvement on the clinch knot and not surprisingly is called the improved clinch knot. This knot has an 85% strength rating. Instead of a single strand of monofilament around the eye of the swivel, the improved clinch features two. (See diagram)

Improved Clinch Knot

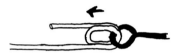

1. Run the line throught the eye of the hook.

2. Make six to eight wraps around the line, and pass tag end through loop.

3. Moisten and pull snug.

The strongest knot I have ever come across was developed by tyee fishermen up in British Columbia ("tyee" means any Chinook salmon over thirty pounds). The knot is called the Rivers Inlet Knot, and anyone familiar with that name knows that is where some of the largest salmon in the world are caught. Guides on the inlet have used this knot for decades, because to land these huge fish requires a knot that holds up under tremendous strain. This is the author's favorite knot, and in all the time spent steelhead fishing, I have never seen this knot break before the line itself! The Rivers Inlet knot has a strength rating of 95%. It is also the best knot I have found to use on lures and plugs. (See diagram.)

Rivers Inlet Knot

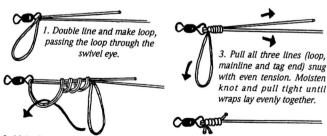

1. Double line and make loop, passing the loop through the swivel eye.

2. Make four wraps around both mainline and tag end, then pass loop through the first.

3. Pull all three lines (loop, mainline and tag end) snug with even tension. Moisten knot and pull tight until wraps lay evenly together.

4. Trim. The Rivers Inlet Knot has a 95% breaking strength.

Practice these knots so they can be performed streamside without a second thought and they will serve you faithfully.

4.) Choosing A Weighting System.

Today, there are basically two choices for getting terminal gear to river bottoms where steelhead lurk. One, you can choose different styles of lead, pencil lead, either hollow-core or solid in 1/4 and 3/16th inch diameter; bank (bell) sinkers from 1/4 to 4 ounces, or "cannon-ball" round style, from one ounce to as heavy as conditions call for. Two, there is the slinky, which is essentially lead shot-filled nylon cord, an almost snagless wonder of the drift fishing world that can be adjusted to almost any river fishing situation by either length or size of shot.

The toughest question that arises when discussing river conditions is determining which weighting system to choose. I would dare to estimate that under 50% of all holding water situations, regardless of time of year, either pencil lead or slinkies will do equally well. The answers to this question depend on the individual angler. There are untold numbers of steelheaders that will not part with their pencil lead. The same can be said for those who fish nothing but a slinky. As in any aspect of steelhead fishing, if an angler is successful with his/her favorite weighting system, by all means stay with it. A rational decision can be tough to make when opinions, favoritism, habit and tradition cloud the mind.

However, varying river situations and conditions can be fished with greater efficiency by switching to a different weighting system. Lead is versatile in its many forms, and slinkies can be adjusted in cord length and shot diameter to fit a myriad of conditions. Still, there will always be a time and place on a steelhead river where one weighting system will out-perform the other.

The only way to do it diplomatically is to analyze river conditions— holding water, temperature, clarity, volume and bottom structure—only then will you know which system to use.

Let's start by individually analyzing the two most practical weighting systems, lead and slinkies, and discuss the advantages and disadvantages of each in varying river conditions. We will break down each one, showing styles of both and give suggestions for their rigging.

First, let's examine the slinky. This revolutionary drift fishing marvel exploded onto the steelheading scene around 1984, but it had been in use, albeit quietly, in Oregon since 1965. The slinky is simply round lead shot stuffed into hollow, dark green nylon cord and melted at both ends. Why it took so long for the slinky to gain in popularity is a mystery. When fishermen first discovered this new weight system, it immediately gave them something that was unknown with pencil lead: maximum sensitivity. This was due to its flexibility. Nylon cord, being slick by nature, does not stick to rocks like lead does. By following the contours of the river bottom, seductively sliding over rocks instead of banging off them (the primary problem with lead), little feel was lost. This meant quite a bit to the steelheader, especially when he was dealing with soft biting fish in cold water situations.

The slinky gives two immediate advantages to the drift fisherman, besides increased sensitivity and its unwillingness to snag up. One, the slinky does not abrade, rough up or nick monofilament like lead does. After only a few drifts, lead becomes rough from banging and scraping off rocks. A fact of drift fishing is that when casting (actually fishing, reeling in and retrieving terminal gear from snags), leaders and mainlines tend to wrap temporarily

The author chose a magnum slinky for use over a large boulder bottom in 50 degree water, with silver results.

around or brush occasionally against weights. The slinky has a body of soft nylon that does not abrade line. Two, because the slinky does not stick and grab rock, it results in a smoother drift. When using pencil lead, an angler must repeatedly jerk on the rod to pull the lead out of the rocks to keep it drifting with the current and keep it from hanging up. Each time the gear is yanked like this, two things happen that do a fisherman no good. One, if you are a bait fisherman, you will pull all or the majority of the bait off with this sudden motion. Two, you pull your drift out of its original position, which will cost fishing time by having to recast to properly cover the water. Also, sudden jerky motions spook steelhead in low, clear, warm water (46 to 60 degrees).

The slinky is endearing to beginning drift fishermen. Trying to get the feel of all the subtle nuances of drift fishing (rocks, sand, a steelhead bite, etc.) can be exasperating to a beginner if his gear is hanging up constantly. It's because he has not yet learned to pull that snaggy piece of lead out of harm's way when it starts to settle in the rocks. Because a slinky is so forgiving, the only feel the beginner has to get used to is a shuffle off the bottom and the sharp take of a steelhead.

There is no doubt that the slinky is a revolutionary drift fishing tool. The trick is knowing and recognizing when to take advantage of it. To do that, we have to look at what types of river situations call for a slinky. First, all you have to do is remind yourself of the slinky's greatest advantage—it slides easily over rocks.

Late winter (February-March) is the time for large native fish. March 10th was the day Salmon-Trout-Steelheader editor Nick Amato tamed this 18 lb. Quinault River male.

Therefore, any stretch of water that features large boulders or any uneven rock configurations (such as clay ledges) that make up an irregular bottom structure are prime areas for slinkys. A standard rule to remember is, anytime you run into basketball-sized rocks (or larger) that make up 80% of the bottom structure, use a slinky.

The snagless feature of the slinky makes it a perfect searching tool in any water temperature, at any time of year. It is the perfect tool when fishing unfamiliar new water or relearning a stretch of river or holding water that may have changed with the high flows of winter. The forgiving nature of a slinky allows you to come in contact with the bottom a little more often during a drift than you should, allowing you to get the feel of the new drift much sooner without donating time and gear to tackle-eating spots. A terminal outfit (weight, swivel, leader, drift bobber, hook) rigged with a

slinky is the ticket until you become familiar with the river.

Now let's look at two different times of year and two completely different water conditions, and see how a slinky can help you work this type of holding water with the greatest efficiency.

First we'll look at winter. Winter means occasional heavy rainfall that can push water levels way up and visibility down. This higher, off-colored water (off-colored meaning still driftable, from 12 inches to 2 feet of visibility) changes steelhead behavior. High, dark water causes them to seek out slower portions of the holding water off to the sides of the increased heavy flow and to search out holding areas with less silt. This slower, less silty water will also be a degree or two warmer than the main flow, which a cold water steelhead will gravitate to. You will always find these conditions relatively close to the bank. This slower, clearer strip of water can be one to 10 feet wide, depending on the bottom structure and placement of the current break or parting line. This is the area where the current changes from swift to soft flow.

To properly drift this water you must present the terminal gear slowly. High winter water is typically cold (35 to 42 degrees), and this means lethargic steelhead. Any presentation moving too swiftly in the reduced visibility, even a bait traveling the same speed as the current inside the slow edge you are targeting could be missed by a steelhead. You must let the terminal setup slip slowly downstream without hanging up, while being able to hold the bottom in the heavier flow. A lead weight does the job well, holding bottom in particular, but the nod has to go to a slinky which will not hang up, whereas the lead may when fishing this slow. The largest style slinky is the choice: the magnum style ("magnum" when referring to slinkies describes the largest diameter shot in the widest nylon cord) with "00" sized lead shot.

When fishing slow, off-colored water with a magnum slinky, rig it up sliding style. In slow, cold, off-colored water, the take of a steelhead is usually soft or simply a stop, and the sliding weight allows for increased feel. There is a direct line from hook to rod tip, without any heavy weight to deaden or absorb the feel of a light pickup.

When fishing large, open rivers (such as the Thompson, Skeena, Snake, Clearwater or Skagit) that have strong, deep flows and large rock/boulder bottoms, the magnum slinky is still the choice. Any large river qualifies that has long, deep (6 to 12 foot) sections of holding water. The large diameter slinky will allow you to make long, extended drifts in this big water without fear of repeatedly hanging up. One tangible to bear in mind before choosing the slinky in a big river situation, is to take a water temperature reading. The feature that makes slinkies non-snaggy (nylon cord) makes them travel at a faster clip than lead. If the temperature is between 45 and 58 degrees, stick with the slinky. Steelhead in this warmer winter condition will be quite active, and a slow moving bait will not be necessary. If the water is colder (33 to 42 degrees), and you must fish slower to allow the more lethargic steelhead time to react to the presentation, go with a dense lead weight. We will cover this in more detail shortly.

Now let's jump to summer conditions. In late spring, summer and early fall, most non-glacial streams will be warmer (48 to 60 degrees), and steelhead metabolism will be at its peak. A faster presented bait will be the norm for these conditions. This is because rivers are usually at their lowest flows of the year, and steelhead will be laying in shallower (2 to 5 feet deep) head-ins or riffles, at the top end of flat sections of holding water. In this swifter flowing water, your bait/drift bobber will be moving at, or slightly slower than, current speed. This is slinky water. When fishing for steelhead with high metabolism, a natural drift is necessary, as lead is much too grabby under these conditions. A slinky is the choice, not only for not spooking those hair-trigger wary fish (they will be alarmed by jerking the bait unnaturally through the drift each time the lead grabs bottom), but also

Slinky Rigs

Unlike lead, there are only two practical ways to rig the slinky: sliding (top) with snap swivel, or fixed to the snap swivel, non-sliding (bottom).

because riffles at head-ins of holding water are always the grabbiest portions of the river, with the largest rocks and boulders. You want the presentation to "glide" (see Chapter Four, Gliding) over the rocks in the long, fast riffles, and the slinky will allow you to do that. This type of holding water, low flows with shallow riffles, requires the smallest diameter slinky. The smaller the shot used, the better.

Times and places on the river for slinky use are: shallow, fast riffles and runs; cold, off-color, slow water; as a searching and familiarizing weight; as a tool for the beginning drift fisherman; and in larger rivers with long, deep stretches of holding water.

The question that arises is always, "How large and what type of slinky do I need?" Impossible to answer here. The only way is to judge for yourself streamside. This is not a cop-out, there is no way to predict the exact amount of weight needed for each water condition and river situation. The best way to prepare is to make slinkies in various lengths and shot diameters as you anticipate needing for your fishing trip. Make your adjustments on the river. Bring along a lighter and small pair of scissors. Only prevailing conditions dictate style and size of slinky to use, and only on-the-river experience can teach that.

Now let's examine the drift fisherman's versatile and nostalgic terminal sinker: lead. There are three types of lead available to the drift fisherman: 3/16ths and 1/4 inch hollow-core and solid pencil lead and bank sinkers. As seemingly infallible as the slinky is, it will never totally replace lead for the drift fisherman. Many steelheaders, especially grizzled veterans, loudly verbalize colorful compound expletives whenever the suggestion is made to give up their precious, faithful pencil lead in favor of the slinky. Lead will always be snaggy, yes, and the angler will always lose more terminal gear when using it, but the advantages lead gives in certain river conditions and situations far outweigh its one disadvantage. There are four specific river conditions/situations in which lead is a key factor in hooking steelhead.

The saving grace for lead is its density. This is the number one reason the slinky has not made this drift fishing dinosaur extinct. With the slinky, no matter how long or heavy (size of lead shot) they are, the nylon casing and long body length catches too much water as it sinks, resulting in a slower sinking weight. This means a terminal slinky outfit needs a few extra feet and a few extra seconds to reach the river bottom. On rivers with long stretches of holding water, this delayed sinking is not a factor in reaching steelhead, but it does bring up the first type of situation that calls for the use of lead.

Here in Washington State, on the Olympic Peninsula, there are several river systems that require slight changes in terminal gear to score consistently. Rivers like the Queets, Quinault, Clearwater (tributary to the Queets) and Hoh all have one thing in common, they are big, fast and powerful. Perhaps you are familiar with these rivers, or another river that is similar. These rivers, and rivers like them are still quite young in geological time; their characteristically wide river beds change with each new flood, sometimes several times a year. These rivers drop many feet per mile on their relatively short run from mountains to ocean, and they are most easily recognized as an unending series of rapids between log jams. Riffle-pool configurations that typify so many steelhead rivers are rare, for these rambunctious waterways are more noted for their crashing, deep runs, swift pockets behind boulders, stumps and downed trees, and deep, swirling cross-currents. Lead is the choice on this type of river.

Because lead is a more concentrated weight than a slinky, it

An angler prepares to make a presentation in green/brown, limited visibility conditions. This lead bank sinker will hold the bobber/bait on the bottom for a slow presentation, necessary in this condition.

sinks more quickly, a major consideration when trying to put a bait in front of a steelhead that noses up tight to one of those obstructions. You must get the offering down *now* to these fish, or the bait will go over their heads and out of their cone of vision. This is especially true in low to normal flows; steelhead will tuck into those hiding places in the clearer water. When the water is running heavy and off-color, the need for lead is not as important, as fish will gravitate to the slow edges. Then you may use a magnum style slinky to reach them. However, in rivers that match this criteria, it would probably be a better choice to stick with lead.

Whenever I fish these rivers, I bring two types of weights with me: magnum slinkies and lead. These rivers really snort when they are running full (not necesarily high, just between normal to high flows) and I usually wind up using lead. Lead holds bottom, allowing for a slower presentation in cold water. The best style of lead to use is one of the two densest styles, the bank (or bell) sinker. Pencil lead (even 1/4 inch) is not dense enough, its long profile catches too much water. Not as much as the slinky, but still sinks too slowly. More importantly, pencil lead does not have enough mass to hold it in a strong current like a bank sinker does. Bank sinkers are concentrated lead. They sink immediately, and this is important when trying to reach nosed-up or swift, deep water steelhead. The bank sinker's compact weight allows for a much more accurate cast, essential when pin-pointing your bait behind an obstruction. Bank sinkers come in a dozen weights, from 1/4 ounce all the way up to 10. The ones most often used in this type of water are 1/2, 3/4, 1, 1-1/2 and 2 ounce. If the situation calls for any weight heavier than this (2 ounces) the water is running too strong for drift fishing, and you need to change techniques (see Chapter Four, Plunking).

Bank sinkers need to be modified or they will be hard to fish. Purchase some vinyl dip, the same stuff that is used to coat the handles on pliers, and dip the bank sinker in up to its eye. (Black dip is best, because it is the least visible to fish.) Hang them up to dry, and create a new, smaller eye above the original (see photo). This smaller eye is where you clip on the sinker, and if it does become hung up, a firm, quick pull will free up the rest of the ter-

minal gear. The vinyl coating keeps the sinker from scraping rocks, eliminating the jerky aspect of lead. You will feel the bank sinker "strumming" the rocks as it travels downstream.

Rig the bank sinker non-sliding on this terminal rig. Sliding rigs tend to ride up onto the mainline when sinking, and it takes a few extra seconds, a few extra feet and a tightening of the line to pull the swivel/leader snug against the sliding weight. There is little feel lost with this setup. The take from a steelhead under these conditions is always strong, due to the split-second decision it has to make to strike in tight holding areas and fast water.

Whenever sliding weights are used, place a 4 or 5 mm plastic bead on the mainline between the swivel and sliding swivel. This protects the knot from abrasion.

The second case for lead is on any stretch of holding water or river that has a clean bottom: rocks not larger than your fist, mixed with intermittent pea-gravel and sand. In this situation, hangups are rare, so lead is a better choice for added sensitivity. Use pencil lead over smooth bottoms. Only the end of the lead will be touching the river bottom, the need for a dense blob of lead doesn't exist. Just the tip of the pencil lead ticking the small rock will provide all the feeling necessary, and it will still allow the terminal gear to travel downstream at, or slightly slower than current speed. Lead gives you more feel in this situation, for sometimes it can be tough to tell bottom or the position of your terminal outfit with a slinky. In areas with large boulders or irregular bottom, it is easy to feel bottom with a slinky. In areas with pea-gravel and small rocks, it isn't. Remember, under these small rock, smoother bottom situations, it is still best to use the smallest, lightest piece of pencil lead available, usually 3/16th inch diameter. You only need to touch bottom a few times during each drift to hook steelhead.

The third case for lead is on small streams. As we discussed in Chapter Two, Reading Water, small stream steelhead are normally limited to any spot that is large enough to hide their bodies. Remember, lead has greater density than a slinky. Lead sinks rapidly, and when fishing small pockets and runs, you have to get the terminal setup down immediately for the fish to see your bait. Pencil lead is the choice in small water, a piece large enough to drop the bait directly to the bottom. Rig the pencil lead directly off a short dropper, non-sliding. You want the bait and lead to reach bottom together. There is no fear of snags with pencil lead in small streams. You will be fishing a short line most of the time (usually a strip and flip sort of cast), simply picking up the line in your free hand and "swing casting" from pocket to pocket. Since the line is short, the lead will rarely have the opportunity to settle beneath a rock and hang up. Most of the makeup of the bottom in a small stream is small rock and gravel. A steelhead take in small water occurs shortly after the bait settles to eye-level, and with a minimum of mainline out, strikes are felt immediately, regardless of the amount of lead needed to swiftly reach bottom.

The fourth case for lead is when "boondogging" or "side-drifting" (see Chapter Four, Techniques). When employing these techniques, immediately knowing where bottom is provides the key to the presentation. A sure indicator is the hard thump of lead against rock. A tiny piece of pencil lead, either 1/4 or 3/16th inch in diameter and approximately a half an inch long, is all that is needed. Remember, since you will be drifting with the current when employing these techniques, the current force is negated, and only enough lead to sink the bait to the bottom is needed. The tiny piece of lead is sufficient because the bottom needs to be felt only infrequently. With a slinky, feeling bottom with weights this light is nearly impossible.

A list of conditions and situations for lead includes deep, swift pockets in larger rivers; swirling cross-currents; holding water with a clean, small rock/pea gravel/sandy bottom; small streams; and for boondogging and side-drifting.

As with slinkies, there will always be the question, " What style, how much and how do I rig lead?" Again, it's impossible to answer here. This can only be done after reading the water and determining your weighting system. If lead is the choice, you must break it down further to determine style and amount of lead. On the river experience is the only answer.

There is an alternative weighting system that has been used since the early 1980s, and that is Luhr Jensen's Bouncing Betty. Its round shape, matched with its rubber compound body make this curious weight almost snagless. The only drawback to the Bouncing Betty is because of its fast reaction bounce to rock contact, it tends to speed up the drift. However, due to its snagless feature, it is a great weight to use if you must cast upriver from your position. Bouncing Bettys are available in 1/4, 1/2, 3/4 and one ounce sizes.

Lead Rigs

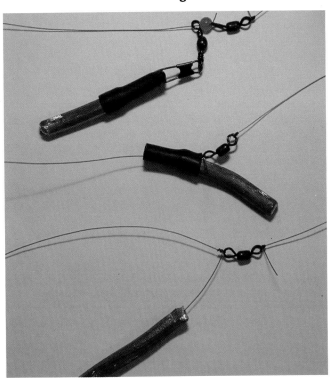

(Top rig) pencil lead with tubing, rigged sliding on a snap swivel (middle rig), pencil lead and tubing slid directly onto the mainline and (bottom rig), hollow-core pencil lead crimped onto a mainline dropper tag.

Sliding Dropper Rigs

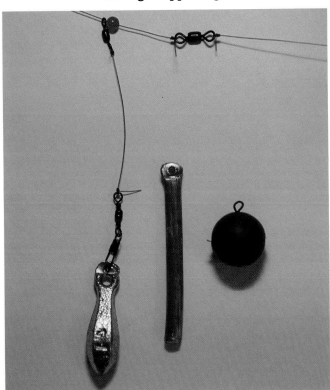

Lead has several shapes, and many ways to rig it. The photo on the left shows a sliding dropper with (left to right): a bank sinker, punched pencil lead, and a Bouncing Betty.

Lead Rigs

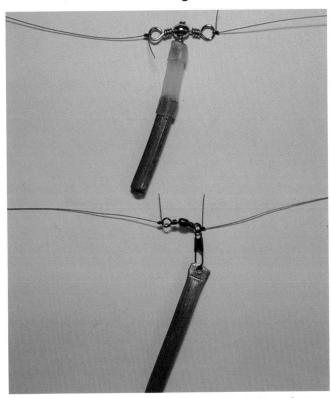

(Top rig) pencil lead inserted into tubing, and attached to a three-way swivel and, (bottom rig) pencil lead punched and clipped onto a snap swivel.

5.) Terminal Setups and Matching Them To River Condition

Leaders

Before diving into matching terminal outfits to conditions, our first job is to select the proper leader. A leader by definition here is the length of monofilament between hook and swivel/weight. Always use a leader that is lighter than the mainline. In case of the hook/drift bobber hanging up, only that portion will be lost if you must break off. Using the same pound test for leader as mainline can result in losing many yards of line on a breakoff.

It is important to choose a brand of line that is low stretch, high knot strength, and abrasion resistant. Lines with hard finishes are the ones to use for leader material. Leaders come in frequent contact with rocks, so a soft monofilament will abrade much faster than a hard one. Low stretch lines allow you to feel light pickups more easily, and allow for quicker hooksets with more transferred force. Also, because your leader is a pound or two lighter in breaking strength than the mainline, high knot strength is doubly important. The leader, being a short length of line with little stretch, must be able to take the repeated shocks of a hookset and a charging steelhead.

Before fishing, choose a brand of line that matches the style of drift technique you plan to use. When fishing spinning drift bobbers, use a brand of monofilament that is a little stiffer. Spinning

bobbers tend to twist leaders that are too limp. Soft monos, when used with spinning drift bobbers, develop kinks that will severely weaken the leader. When fishing lighter pound test leaders and bait with small drift bobbers, use a softer brand of line. The softer mono allows the bait to drift with a more natural action and is not nearly as detectable by a fish on a gentle pickup.

Color of monofilament is important when choosing a line for leader material. Pick one that is a natural tone, either brown or green. Then match the leader color to the river conditions. A leader that matches the surroundings will blend in with the background and not alarm steelhead. Does the river have a dark bottom with a tea-stain color to it? Choose a brown tone line for leader. Does the river have a light bottom with clear/green water? Choose a leader with a green tint. The best color choice for leaders in any situation would be a green tint line, because it is the most natural color in all river surroundings, winter and summer. In the opinions of many guides and old-timers, green is the very best color choice for leaders. An excellent compromise when fishing an unfamiliar river would be to use a clear line for leaders, as clear would adapt to any condition.

How long a leader is practical? This depends on present water conditions. You want to use the shortest possible leader for the conditions. Why the shortest leader? For example, if you were using a 2 foot leader, by the time a steelhead picks up your offering, the weight has had to travel double the length of the leader before the mainline tightens and the bite is felt. (Keep in mind the whole time your weight is traveling, the fish is trying to spit out the sharp, painful object in its jaw.) That means the weight must travel 4 feet before anything is felt. Shorten that leader to 18 inches, and it only has to travel 3 feet before the bite is felt. Now, if a steelhead just hauls off and whaps the bait, leader length means nothing, but when a fish simply stops the offering as they are so notoriously known to do, the shortest possible leader will allow the angler to feel the pickup sooner. The sooner the bite is felt, the less time a steelhead has to eject the hook.

Leader length is determined by degrees of visibility. Ideally, the steelhead should see only the drift bobber/bait coming downstream, not the swivel/weight. In conditions where there is some color in the water, only the brightness of the drift bobber/yarn/bait will be noticed to any degree, due to minimal light penetration. A steelhead will not see a dark swivel/weight before the bobber/bait. Therefore, a short leader is the order. Twelve inches should be the minimum length, to allow bobbers/bait enough leeway to ride up away from the rocks, and to keep the gear legal (many regulations state that a hook may be no closer to a weight than 12 inches). When fishing cloudy or colored water, ideal leader length is between 18 and 22 inches.

In water with slight color (4 feet visibility) to unlimited/clear, separation of bobber/bait and swivel/weight is more important. Colors of bobber/bait will be subtle and smaller. Ideal leader length for clearer water conditions will be between 24 and 34 inches.

Small streams will be a deviance from the norm. Regardless of water conditions, a short leader is always used in tight-quarter fishing. The idea in small streams is to get the bait to the steelhead immediately, and this is done best with a leader that is no longer than 13 inches. I have caught steelhead in tiny streams with an 8 inch leader and found no reduction in strikes because of it. However, there are regulations concerning the minimum amount of leader length on many streams. This law is put into effect on many waters to prevent or discourage snagging. As always, check the legal minimum on leader length before you fish.

Pip's

Pre-tie all leaders at home. This will save you immeasurable amounts of time streamside, as all the effort spent attaching leader to hook will mean wasted fishing time. An hour is normally all the time you need to sit down and tie up a few dozen leaders. There are a couple of ways to carry leaders. One way is wrapped around a leader card, but the leaders and bumper knots may suffer from abrasion during transportation (banging around in a vest pocket, for example). The best item for leader storage is the "Pip's" leader dispenser. This round dispenser has a soft cork center that stores hooks without dulling them and will hold approximately 40 leaders up to 36 inches long. Dispensers can be labeled for identification, and they fit smartly into a vest pocket. "Pip's" dispensers are manufactured by Mack's Lures, P.O. Box 507, Leavenworth, Washington, 98826. Dial 1-(509) 548-5716.

The Importance of Yarn

Yarn, either natural or fluorescent colored, has been in the drift fisherman's arsenal since the 1930s. Placed above the hook or more commonly tied in an overhand knot in the egg loop of a bumper knot, yarn is a standard part of the terminal outfit. The addition of yarn (called "wool" by British Columbia steelheaders, all yarn sold commercially for steelheading today is made from spun polyester) to the hook does more than enhance a drift lure. Yarn has four important functions for the drift fisherman.

Yarn

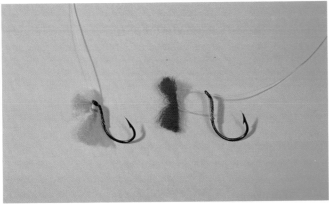

This photo shows properly rigged yarn tied into the "egg loop" of the hook. Yarn gives two advantages to the angler: one, the yarn momentarily sticks in the teeth of the steelhead and two, yarn keeps the line from cutting through the bait.

First, it acts as a strike detector, the nature of yarn with its intertwined fibers catch in the many small teeth in the mouth of a steelhead. This can prevent the fish from immediately ejecting the hook after it picks up the drift lure. This extra second of grace to feel the bite may mean the difference between hooking the fish and missing it altogether. Second, yarn adds color and enhances the profile of the drift bobber or bait. This is important in low light, or water conditions with restricted visibility and color. Third, yarn is a bait protector. The knot of yarn in the bait loop of the bumper knot prevents line from cutting through delicate baits, such as cluster eggs and sand shrimp. These hard to obtain baits will last for several additional drifts when used with yarn in the egg loop. Lastly, yarn can be used solo as an attractor lure. Yarn flies are nothing more than two to a half dozen colors of yarn tied into the bumper knot loop, or tied above the eye of the hook. Yarn flies are very effective in low water situations.

Two additional things to remember when using yarn. One,

Yarn

Two ways of tying yarn drift lures.

when tying yarn into the egg loop, leave the trailing "wings" of yarn no longer than the bottom of the hook. Yarn that has long tails on it will not lessen the amount of strikes from steelhead, but those same steelhead may nip at those long tails and miss the hook entirely. I've seen it happen, folks. Trim the wings of the yarn 1/2 inch to one inch long maximum, even on #3/0 hooks. This is the most yarn you will ever need on a drift lure. Remember, never let the yarn hang below the bend of the hook.

Second, to add to the sticky aspect that yarn has with steelhead teeth, there are a few things you can do. When tying in the yarn, do not comb or separate the strands of yarn. It may look prettier, but the yarn won't stick as well if the fibers are pulled apart. To make the yarn really grab, tie an additional overhand knot on each one of the wings. Do this by starting with a section of yarn approximately 8 inches long. After tying the overhand knot (in the egg loop) in the middle of the length of yarn, tie an additional overhand knot in each wing approximately one inch or less from the original knot in the line loop. Pull the knots as tight as possible. Trim the yarn flush with the knots so the knots themselves are the ends of the wings. Now you have made your yarn a real tooth-snagger. When a steelhead picks up this knotted yarn, its teeth cannot pull through the yarn—the knots on the ends prevent it. Steelhead have a tough time spitting this lure out. (See photo)

Yarn

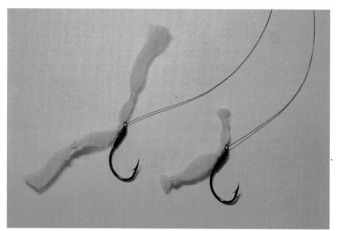

Yarn momentarily hangs up in a steelhead's mouth, however, knotted yarn catches teeth for a longer period, giving the angler even more time to set the hook.

When using yarn, either solo or as an added attractor on a bait/drift bobber, use two different colors for contrast. In theory, contrasting colors look more like natural feed for steelhead when they are out in the open ocean. More than that, contrasting yarn colors are more easily noticed, especially in limited visibility conditions. Use a light color next to a darker one. For example, use white with hot pink, chartreuse with orange, light pink with rocket red, etc. Yarn should always be an automatic addition to the terminal outfit.

There is one very effective drift lure for steelhead that should be in every angler's vest, and it's the Glo-Bug. (See photo) Not a drift bobber, but made entirely of brand-name Glo-Bug yarn, this single salmon egg imitation has a large following among California steelheaders, but is equally effective wherever anadromous rainbows are found. Commonly tied on sizes #4 and #2 hooks, the Glo-Bug is effective in low, clear water conditions. Always fished solo on 6 or 8 pound test leader, the Glo-Bug looks translucent when in the water, giving it the look of a real egg. If you are proficient in fly tying, you may make these yourself. If not, they are available at almost any fly fishing shop, sporting goods outlet, or directly from The Bug Shop of Anderson, California, (916)-365-1368.

Yarn (Glo-Bugs)

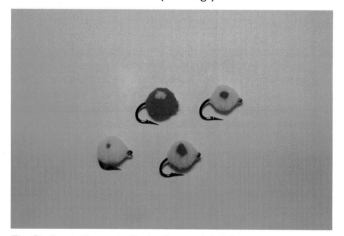

The Glo Bug is the most effective "yarn only" drift lure. The body of the Glo Bug looks translucent in the water, closely resembling a real egg.

6.) Matching Water Conditions

Remember earlier in the chapter when favorite terminal riggings was the topic? Each steelheader has a favorite combination of hook style/colors of yarn/color, style and size of drift bobber/leader/swivel/style of weight that consistently catches fish. Under approximately 80% of all river conditions, an angler could use one combination and have a good chance of getting a hookup. Here lies the problem. Fishermen that stubbornly stay with one specific terminal outfit cheat themselves out of more hookups by refusing to change to a more effective setup for different conditions.

One of the most important keys to successful steelhead drift fishing (besides reading water) is *flexibility*. Let's look at a hypothetical situation between two anglers and see the importance of being flexible about terminal outfits for river conditions.

Angler A fishes nothing but large, #6 chartreuse Spin-N-Glo's, #3/0 hooks and 15 pound test leaders. Steelheader B fishes nothing but tiny #14 pink-pearl Cheaters, #2 hooks and 6 pound test. First, we will drop them both onto a summer river. Conditions are low and clear, water temperature 58 degrees. Steelhead are extremely active; warm water has their metabolism sky high. It will take very little size, color or motion of the terminal outfit to attract them and make them strike.

Angler A and B both cast and make a presentation. What happens? Since the steelhead are hair-trigger wary in their clear water holding spot and the warm water has their body metabolism revved up, the large, gaudy Spin-N-Glo and easily seen, heavy leader of fisherman A will send every fish in the drift fleeing in terror. A large profile, brightly-colored lure shocks steelhead in these conditions. Only the very odd fish will take this offering, and probably only in very fast water in low-light conditions of early morning or evening. Fisherman B, on the other hand, with his small profile, low-toned natural colored Cheater, small hook and light, imperceptible leader will not alarm a wary steelhead in the warm, clear water. This terminal setup has just enough color and profile to attract fish without spooking them.

Now let's take angler A and B and drop them onto a winter river. Water conditions will be slightly high with some color, 2 feet of visibility, water temperature 38 degrees. Because the water is cold, the fish will be a bit lethargic, and the limited visibility will give steelhead a sense of security. They will not be spooky. In these conditions, it will take a drift lure with increased action to make a lethargic fish respond and strike, and the lack of visibility calls for a larger profile lure with a bright colored finish to increase the fish's sight radius. In other words, the bigger and brighter the lure, the easier it is for sight restricted fish to find it. Fisherman B can certainly hook steelhead under these conditions with his tiny Cheater and light gear, but due to the drift bobber's subtle colors and small profile, it will require a lot more casts to work the water thoroughly enough for the fish to find it. Also, higher water means heavier water. Light lines and leaders make it difficult to control a steelhead when it uses the swifter, increased flows to its advantage. Angler A, with his brightly colored, large profile Spin-N-Glo, will excite lethargic fish to strike and require fewer casts to work a section of holding water. The heavier 15 pound test will help control a steelhead in the increased flows.

Now it should be a bit clearer to you concerning the importance of flexibility when steelhead drift fishing. Each fisherman could have greatly improved his chances for a hookup in each situation if he would have simply swapped terminal riggings or adjusted them to the conditions.

As we did in Chapter Two, we will not be discussing terminal outfits for winter and summer steelhead seperately. A steelhead will not hit a certain drift bobber or bait because it is a summer or winter fish. Not species, but present river conditions dictate which outfit the fish strike. They all react the same to given water height, temperature and clarity. These three variables are what we will be concentrating on in this portion of the chapter. They will dictate which color, size and style of drift bobber; size of hook; colors of yarn; length, color, degree of stiffness and pound test of leader are most effective.

Rigs for Water Conditions

Four examples of matching rigs to conditions, from left: low and clear; three to four feet of visibility; two to three feet of visibility; and twelve inches to two feet of visibility.

Now that we understand steelhead behavior, we will match terminal outfits as they apply to driftable water conditions. Driftable conditions are primarily dependent on water clarity. As long as there is a minimum of 12 inches of visibility, drift fishing for steelhead is a viable option. Determining terminal outfits depends most on degrees of visibility, to a lesser degree water volume, and least in importance, water temperature.

When West Coast steelhead rivers first start to recede from high, brown, roily and unfishable, there will be the initial signs of driftability—brownish-green to white-green water with approximately a foot of visibility, along with continuing heavy water volume. Limited visibility and limited lighting call for the brightest, largest drift bobbers, baits, hooks and heavier leaders. Drift bobbers should be large and have action to add vibration to help steelhead find the offering. Spinning drift bobbers are the best choice in heavy, colored water. The Spin-N-Glo in sizes 4, 6 and 8, and the Flash and Spin Cheater in sizes 4 and 2 are ideal for this condition. Colors should be as bright as possible. The glow-in-the-dark finish is the best choice, followed by chartreuse/glow, chartreuse/white or hot pink/glow. Black-winged drift bobbers should be considered, for black produces the best silhouette, and can be seen in limited visibility conditions almost as well as glow-in-the-dark and chartreuse. Yarn colors follow suit, with glow-in-the-dark, (there are glow yarns now on the market) chartreuse/white, chartreuse/black and char-

treuse/hot pink. Chartreuse and glow-in-the-dark are the best colors to use, either in drift bobbers or yarn combinations, because they can be seen in low to zero light conditions. Bait should always be used, when legal, in high, colored water to assist the fish in finding the lure. Bait puts out a cone of scent in the water below the lure and increases the lure's profile.

To maximize the effectiveness of the glow-in-the-dark finish on the drift bobber, purchase a flash unit to charge the phosphorescence. By charging the drift bobber with the flash, it will glow an intense green for several minutes, much brighter and longer than if using only natural light or a flashlight. In limited visibility conditions, charging up the glow in drift bobbers will give an added attraction radius.

Hooks need to be large. With the use of larger drift bobbers comes the need to increase the hold area of the hook gap. Numbers #2/0 and #3/0 match drift bobber size, and larger hooks also help hold a steelhead in swifter, higher water. Having to put more pressure on a steelhead when it gets into increased flows means fish will tear loose unless there is plenty of hook gap holding its jaw.

Leaders should be shorter, with a heavier pound test. As always, when using spinning drift bobbers, use a stiff monofilament. Leader color is never a factor in dark, colored water. A steelhead cannot see bailing wire in dark water. Twelve pound should be the lightest used and only if the fish can be chased for some distance. More practical pound tests for this condition are 15 to 17. These two weights suffice for almost any high water situation. Because the water is darker and visibility is limited, leader length should be between 16 to 20 inches.

When rivers drop from brown/white-green to dark green, with a foot and a half to two and a half feet of visibility, lighting and visibility will still be limited and water volume substantial. Large, bright drift bobbers, baits and hooks and moderately heavy leaders are still the order. Spinning drift bobbers, with their wobbling/vibrating action, will still produce best. Spin-N-Glo's in sizes 6 and 8, Flashing-Spinning Cheaters in 4 and 6, and Birdies in 3 and 5 are the top choices. Colors should still be bright; with chartreuse, chartreuse/fire orange, hot pink/white, and hot pink/black excellent selections. Yarn colors should contrast with drift bobber colors: chartreuse with hot pink, white or fire orange; and pink/white. Bait should also be added; its profile and scent always help in limited visibility.

Hooks should be large. Size #2/0 is ideal for controlling steelhead in heavier flows. Leaders will be moderately heavy and short, and stiff monofilament is still the order with spinning drift bobbers. Line color is still not a factor for leaders, as visibility is still limited. Twelve to 15 pound test is most practical and, due to restricted visibility, an 18 to 22 inch leader will suffice.

When steelhead rivers have that "dialed-in" green look, the color that every angler drools over, there will be 2-1/2 to 4 feet of visibility. These conditions create a gray area. Due to increased light penetration in the water, there will be a wider variance of colors, drift bobbers, hooks, yarn and baits that work most efficiently. If you have a favorite combination terminal outfit that attracts steelhead under most conditions, chances are good it will work when the river shows this degree of coloring. The author's all-time favorite drift bobber style/color comes from this condition, the #2, pink "nail polish" finished Okie. Confidence had as much to do with the tremendous success of that color/style drift bobber as anything. However, there are some guidelines that should be followed.

The author's favorite drift bobber, the old-style "nail-polish" light pink Okie. Confidence and proper presentation made this drift bobber as successful as any other color or style of bobber.

Drift bobber size shrinks, colors need not be so bright, and do not need as much action imparted to them. Pound test of leaders drops, and so does hook size. Wobbling bobbers are the best choice, however; spinning bobbers in smaller sizes are also effective. Spinning drift bobbers like the Spin-N-Glo in sizes 8 and 10, the Spinning Cheater in 6 and 8, and Birdies in sizes 1 and 3 are the choice; in wobbling bobbers, the Okie in sizes 2 and 3, and the Cheater in 10 and 8; and non-action bobbers like the Corkie in sizes 8 and 10. Colors can be bright to natural tones, but this choice depends largely on the weather. Overcast, dark days call for brighter drift bobber colors: hot pink, fire orange, lime/orange or hot pink/white. (White can also be classified as pearl, but there

are some drift bobbers that are definitely white.) Yarn combinations should follow closely, with hot pink/white, hot orange/white, yellow/hot pink or fire orange/hot pink.

On bright days, with light, high clouds or sunny skies, comes the need to tone down the colors. With added light penetration, there is no need for brighter colors to get the attention of steelhead. As in any steelheading technique, you want to attract without alarming the fish. Jed Davis first coined the phrase "attraction threshold" in his book *"Spinner Fishing for Steelhead, Salmon and Trout."* This theory is a strong one: you want to get the most aggressive response out of the steelhead without spooking it. While the brighter colors may be fine for darker days under this condition, with the added light of the sun on a bright day, those same colors may spook fish. Be sure to use a different color yarn scheme than the one(s) in the drift bobber. In this condition, you still want to create a drift lure with contrast. Colors for this increased lighting will be pink/pearl (pink spot or solid color), orange/pearl, metallic blue/orange, metallic pink, sunrise (a lighter orange), or pink/black spot. Yarn colors will be the same, with pink/white, yellow/white, orange/white, orange/yellow, hot pink/light pink, or pink/black. Bait will still be an added attractant, but bait sizes will be made smaller. As you can see, the color combinations of drift bobber/yarn are many, and any of the colors mentioned will hook fish in this "dialed-in" condition.

Hooks should be big, but not as large as the higher water sizes. Sizes #1/0 and #2/0 match drift bobber sizes well and will be plenty of hook to hold a fish in moderate flows. Leader color now becomes a factor, as some rivers (mostly non-glacial) will have a definite tea-stain color, while others (usually of all or some glacial origin) will be predominantly green in color. Match leader

Pink is the best all-condition color for steelhead drift fishing. This 18 lb. buck picked up a #10 pink Corkie, pink/white yarn and eggs.

color to the river color, or go with a neutral, clear monofilament for leader material. Twelve and 10 pound test are the most practical for this condition, and because of increased visibility, leaders should be slightly longer, between 20 and 24 inches.

When steelhead rivers are at their clearest and running at stable to low flows, visibility will be 4 feet to gin clear. Now that there is maximum light penetration, drift gear must be toned down accordingly. Drift bobbers should be small, colors natural, and in gin clear conditions bobbers are now an option. Yarn colors no longer need to contrast and are also predominantly natural. Leaders will be their lightest and longest, performing best when line color is matched to the river. Hooks and baits will also be sized down. The smallest drift bobbers work best: Corkies in #14, 12 and 10; Okies in sizes 1 and 2 and Cheaters in 14 and 12. The smallest spinning bobbers can also be used and are the better choice in low, clear, colder water conditions common during winter months. The number 14 Spin-N-Glo and #10 Flashing Spinning Cheater are best. Drift bobber colors will be pink/pearl (pink spotted or solid color), light orange, red (commonly called "rocket red", it looks like a San Francisco 49er home jersey), purple, blue/pearl, metallic blue, light pink, sunrise, lime green, light pink, black or light pink/black spot. Black drift bobbers are best when the water is warmer (54 to 62 degrees) and clear. Black suggests a presence of a lure without any color to alarm fish. Yarn colors closely follow, though contrast to attract the attention of steelhead is unnecessary due to unlimited visibility and maximum light penetration. The best yarn colors are light pink, pink/white, light orange, white, red, red/white or yellow.

Hooks are smaller, with #1/0 being the largest, and #1 and #2 more accurately matching drift bobber size, line weight and size of bait. Line pound test will vary from 10 pound in faster water with a tinge of color, to 8 and 6 pound in low, clear conditions. Using a larger hook, a #2/0 for example, will not necessarily cut down on the number of takes in clearer water but would instead be harder to set with a light leader. For example, the force transfer needed to set the full tine of a #2/0 into the hard mouth of a steelhead can break six pound test. Eight or 10 pound test should be the lightest leader for practical use with a #2/0 hook.

In maximum visibility conditions, leader color should match water/bottom color so as not to tip off steelhead that something is hanging off the drift lure. Bait will always help attract strikes, and since visibility is unlimited, the smallest baits are all that is necessary.

I have never been in a condition where dropping below 6 pound test leader was necessary to hook steelhead. Unless you use a noodle rod and have a lot of real estate available to chase a hooked fish, trying to land a powerful fish like a steelhead on anything less than 6 pound test is a bad idea. Except for a few isolated techniques, the best tip is to use the heaviest pound test for

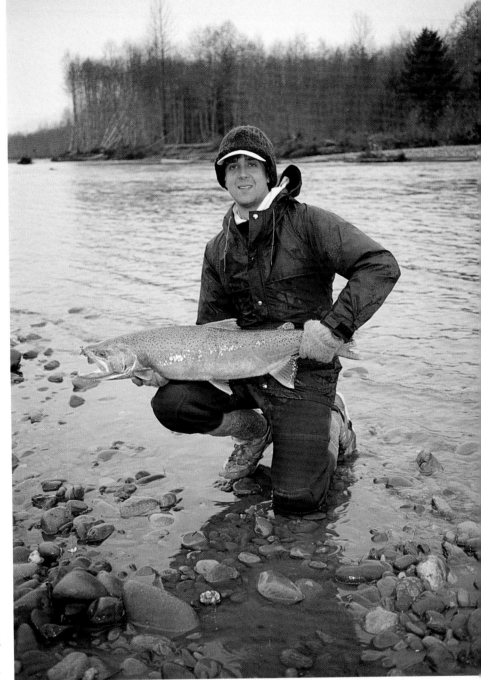

This fifteen-pound Olympic Peninsula native slammed a "trophy" terminal rigging.

the conditions and still get strikes. Rarely, in any situation, summer or winter, will I drop below 8 pound test. There is no reduction in the number of takes, and you never know when "Ike" is going to pick up your offering. ("Ike" is the name given to the biggest damned steelhead in the river.) Six pound test or less will not give you much chance at that trophy fish, unless you are very lucky.

Which colors are the best all-around steelhead attractors? Except for off-colored, limited visibility, light resricted conditions where glow-in-the-dark and chartreuse are needed for attracting the attention of steelhead, there are a few basic colors that will do the job in all water conditions, summer or winter. Tackle manufacturers may not agree, but a drift fisherman only needs three colors to entice a steelhead. They are, in order of preference: pink, white and black. This may seem too simple to be true, but steelhead key on these three colors more than any others. The color pink, either hot pink, medium pink or light pink, accounts for more steelhead strikes per fisherman than any other. This is documented by drift fishermen, fly fishermen and backtrollers of plugs. Why steelhead key on pink is anyone's guess, but they do, and that's all that matters. Many expert steelheaders theorize that most of the steelhead's feed at sea is predominantly pink or white, and that color similarity is the reason for the attraction. For decades fly fishermen have used black as the main color in hundreds of steelhead fly patterns and, to a man, will agree that black is the best color to choose when fly fishing for steelhead. The theory behind black is that most of the food in streams is dark colored, black in particular, and a latent feeding response from the steelhead occurs when it sees a black lure/fly. At any rate, simplicity is always best, and if the drift fisherman stays with these three colors—pink, black and white—he will be as successful as any other angler on the river, and possibly more so.

There are some terminal outfits that do not follow the previous suggestions for matching to conditions. When dealing with large, aggressive native steelhead, terminal gear must be matched to the size and power of the quarry, more than to conditions. Two types of large native fish come to mind: the temporary residents of the big, powerful, fast-flowing rivers on Washington's Olympic Peninsula and British Columbia's Thompson and Skeena Rivers. Steelhead that swim up these systems in late winter and fall, respectively, are the largest, most aggressive steelhead anywhere. Hooking these outsized fish (averaging 15 pounds) is not a problem. They are not line shy and will strike almost any properly presented drift lure/bait, but you need heavy leaders, larger hooks and large drift bobbers to catch them.

Color for the conditions will still be a factor. Drift bobber colors should follow closely the suggested colors for degrees of visibility just covered. Bobbers should be larger, and to appeal to such large steelhead, must have some action imparted to them. The best drift bobbers for trophy steelhead are spinning bobbers; they have the most action and elicit the greatest reaction. A drift bobber, like a plug or spoon, must excite the fish into striking. The Spin-N-Glo in sizes 8 and 6 are the top vote getters, with numbers 4 and 2 for the Flashing Spinning Cheater, and the largest Birdy, the #5, next. If there is a favorite drift bobber that attracts large steelhead for you, by all means don't switch. Keep in mind that my largest steelhead hooked on drift gear sucked in an Okie. For the same reasons that oversize steelhead are taken consistently on backtrolled plugs and spoons, they will hit a large drift bobber, even in clear water conditions. A large fish will not leave its position unless the offering is taken as an intrusion to its space, or is treated as a meal large enough to warrant burning extra energy to nab it.

To hold trophy steelhead and land them quickly so they are not played to exhaustion (and may still be released), hooks in #2/0 and #3/0 are the choice, and leaders that test from 15, 17 and even 20 pound test. Remember, these fish are not line shy, so heavy leaders not only give you a reasonable chance to land a trophy fish, but also aid in landing it more quickly to allow for a harmless release. Steelhead of 20 pounds or better can go just about anywhere they please after being hooked, and giant male steelhead are notorious for finding any or all obstructions in the river. Heavier leaders will help steer the big boys away from them. Leader color is still a factor in clear water conditions. Make sure the leader matches the river color/bottom. Large, aggressive natives may not be line shy, but they are still wary of anything unnatural in clear conditions.

Author's FavoriteTrophy Steelhead Terminal Setup

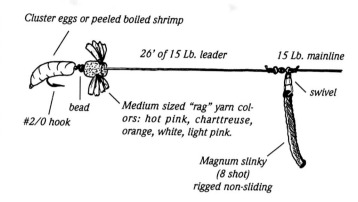

Cluster eggs or peeled boiled shrimp

26' of 15 Lb. leader *15 Lb. mainline*

bead *swivel*

#2/0 hook *Medium sized "rag" yarn colors: hot pink, charttreuse, orange, white, light pink.*

Magnum slinky (8 shot) rigged non-sliding

Matching colors, sizes and styles of drift bobbers; yarn colors; length, pound test and color of leaders; and hook sizes to current river conditions is a big part of the drift fishing puzzle. Putting the pieces together to make the correct terminal outfit will result in many more steelhead hookups.

7.) From Other Techniques: Drifting Flies, Plugs, and Thin-Bladed Spoons

When drift fishing for steelhead, situations occur when the standard terminal outfit will not capture their interest. These three variations of the terminal outfit will draw strikes when seemingly all options are exhausted. You will rarely use these variations, but as with all other steelheading techniques, there will come a condition or holding water situation that calls for their use.

Substituting a fly, plug or thin-bladed spoon for a drift bobber/bait may often be a novel alternative to steelhead, giving them a different look, so to speak, at a lure they have not been subjected to. They will often take a lure that has not stung them, or been presented repeatedly. There is some evidence of this behavior when steelhead are subjected to heavy angling pressure. While this may have some truth to it, the reason a steelhead strikes or picks up a certain lure is related to water and/or weather conditions. We will look at which of these conditions make drifting a fly, plug or thin-bladed spoon a viable choice.

First, the fly and the plug. Why both at once? The reason is they are effective under the exact same conditions. Those conditions are the most common ones found on West Coast rivers during the late summer/early fall, when rivers are at their lowest and warmest flows. Visibility is unlimited and water temperatures will be between 56 to 62 degrees. Summer steelhead in this temperature range are extremely wary. Their body metabolism is also at its peak, so much so that any bait or lure, no matter how small, may spook them. In this situation, fly fishermen often have greater success in triggering strikes than drift fishermen. This is due to the fly's small, dark, natural profile. By simply tying a fly on the end of the leader instead of a drift bobber/bait, gear anglers can reap the same rewards.

Predominantly dark flies, in black and dark browns in sizes 2, 4 and 6 are most effective. Tie them to the lightest leader your gear can stand; a 36 inch length of clear, or green, 6 pound test would be a good choice. Patterns proved productive for drift fishing are hellgrammite and stonefly imitations, black marabou leeches, Woolly Buggers in black and brown and Muddlers (a sculpin imitation). Fish flies exactly as you would with bait. The take on a drifted fly is rarely subtle, most summer runs will take them aggressively.

Fly Rigging

Proper rigging for a fly.

Some summer steelhead that have been in the river for several months will often be "buried" in their holding spots—buried is a term for steelhead that seemingly will not respond to any lure. Steelhead show this behavior when the water temperature gets up around 62 degrees. They are sometimes lying in plain sight, motionless. They will not move unless threatened, thus the "buried" term. Two techniques can wake up these hypnotized fish. One, an angler can swing a spoon in front of the fish, banging the spoon off the rocks to get their attention. This works occasionally, but there is a drifting technique that is more reliable: a plug. Drifting plugs is nothing new, it has been practiced since the Flatfish was introduced in the 1940s and is one of the original methods of steelhead drift fishing. Not just any style of steelhead/salmon plugs are used for backtrolling in rivers, these are a specific style, size and color—the Flatfish, and also the Kwikfish. Both are readily available in a wide market. These plugs have an extreme side-to-side wiggle, much more pronounced than other types of plugs used for steelhead fishing. This animated wobble seems to break a buried steelhead out of its hypnotic state. Steelhead will slam these style plugs when seemingly nothing else will work. They are designed for use in light currents, that is they can be drifted along at slightly slower than current speed (normal drifting speed) which will still impart maximum action. Present the plug with the standard swing. Even for low, clear, warm conditions, use a plug between 4-1/2 to 5 inches long. The U-20 size Flatfish is a perfect size, and the F-11 Kwikfish is comparable. This large plug will swing down and across the holding water with a very pronounced throb transferred to the rod tip. Use a fairly heavy monofilament for the conditions. Steelhead attack these plugs, and light line will not take the shock. Ten or 12 pound test works perfect; the fish are bearing down on the lure and do not notice the line, even in clear water. Plug colors that work best are another oddity. The most effective ones are hot fluorescent orange and, to a lesser degree, chrome with an orange bill. One more note: most plugs in this style come with a treble hook. Switch the treble to a single Siwash for better strike to hookup ratios and to make the plug legal in all waters.

Since these "banana-style" plugs are buoyant, and their design does not allow them to dive for more than a few feet, weight must

be added to the plug, but not much, as the plug will still dive. Only a few split shot carefully squeezed onto the line, or a tiny piece of 1/4 inch pencil lead (approximately 1/2 to 3/4 inch long) placed between two 1/2 inch long pieces of rubber tubing slid onto the line, will help the plug work near the bottom.

Plug Rigging

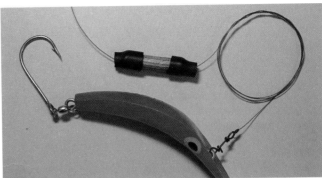

Twelve-pound leader and pencil lead on two small pieces of tubing; th U-20 orange Flatfish.

Finally, let's look at the thin-bladed spoon. Unlike its heavier cousins, steelhead find their anorexic kin just as appealing when drifted on a terminal outfit. A TBS (thin-bladed spoon) is generally small and light, most styles running between 1/16th and 1/8th ounce, and an inch up to 2 inches long. Their thin profile makes them almost neutral in buoyancy, and because they are so thin and light, action is imparted to them at a much higher frequency than a thicker spoon. This gives the TBS a fast, high-action wobble when drifted against the current.

In cold water winter situations (33 to 41 degrees), the added profile and flash of a TBS can elicit strikes from lethargic steelhead, or give steelhead that have been subject to heavy pressure a different look lure. Find TBS's in bright colors and silver plating for best results, the silver plated spoon being the first choice, and the silver/orange head the second. Thin-blades are the only spoon style that should be used in tandem with lead. Whereas adding lead to a normal steelhead spoon would cut down on the action, a TBS has enough action to negate the lead and attract fish. A TBS can be drifted where normal spoon fishing techniques would be impractical. Present the TBS with the standard swing. A drifted thin-bladed spoon, like the fly and plug, can be the answer to the puzzle of getting strikes in difficult conditions where normal drift fishing techniques have failed. (See diagram for TBS rigging.)

TBS Rigging

Small lead and 32 inches of 12 lb. leader, and thin bladed spoon.

CHAPTER 4

TECHNIQUES FOR STEELHEAD DRIFT FISHING

We have discussed the range and run timing of steelhead, reading of water and terminal setups. In Chapter Four we will put this knowledge to use with eight drift fishing techniques, all different yet effective under varying river conditions.

The most important component of any drift fishing technique is positioning: where to start on a section of holding water, where to stand or position your boat, and how to begin the drift. We will also need to know how to present the terminal outfit with the basic swing drift, the drift technique used in 80% of all types of holding water. We will show how to extend the drift and cover more water, and look at four "out of the norm" techniques—driftmending, boondogging, side-drifting, and gliding. Finally, we will see how to solve high, off-color water conditions by plunking and back-bouncing. Matching the proper technique to river conditions is one of the major keys to drift fishing success.

1.) Positioning Equals Success

How you position yourself before starting the presentation will directly affect your success on the river. It's easy to spot a great steelhead fisherman. Watch how he begins fishing a stretch of holding water. Does he go straight to the meat of the water, or does he start above it and patiently work down to it? The successful steelheader will always be the one that begins above the holding area. This is the first rule of proper positioning: always start at the uppermost section of the holding water. This means that almost without exception, you will be working downstream. Sometimes this is impossible, due to inaccessibility of some sections of holding water. There will always be times when the only presentation will be from below the holding area. In this situation, it's better to make a cast from below than not at all. It's more difficult to feel what is happening and avoid snags, but you can still hook fish. However, the proper way to start is to make the first cast into holding water directly above the area you would expect the first steelhead to be holding under the current conditions.

Why start at the very top of the drift and not go directly to the best looking piece of water? For three reasons. First, and probably the most important in any steelheading technique, is that it allows the terminal gear to be worked *in front of* any or all steelhead in the drift. Since a steelhead's greatest range of vision is directly above and in front of it, it can see the bait easier and more quickly. This is important when rivers are running with some color.

Second, there is no chance your mainline or terminal outfit will accidentally rub across a fish from the blind side, alarming it. This happens, folks. Forget about that fish biting. Bumped fish are the result of random casting, or simply making that first cast to the meat of the holding water. Think about it: how many times have you or your partner made a hasty cast dead center in the can't miss water and come up empty? Sure, there may not have been any fish in the drift, but chances are just as good that your terminal gear landed on top of, or very close to the steelhead and spooked it. Start at the very top of the holding water and work down. By doing so, every steelhead (or the only one!) in that section of river will have the bait presented in front of it every time. A thought to live by: the random cast will only hook the random steelhead.

The third reason for starting at the top end of holding water is to take advantage of the steelhead's territorial instincts. It's a fact: when a steelhead has established a holding spot, it will try to remove anything foreign that enters into its area. By having the bait come straight downstream at the fish, you are triggering this territorial response, which typically results in the steelhead simply picking up the offending item and spitting it out of its area. Unfortunately for the fish, this is not always possible. Sometimes the "item" has a hook in it!

Now that you have determined where to begin working the drift, you must decide on a "workable casting distance." This is

Starting at the top and patiently working down through the holding water paid off for Gary Morganthaler. This spring steelhead was the only fish in a 50-yard run.

dictated by current river conditions. If the river is running mild and clear, you want to position yourself as close to the holding area as possible without spooking the quarry. If the water has color, this is not as important. However, you do want to get as close as conditions allow. You want to fish the shortest amount of line and still be able to cover all the water. Have no more line out than you can readily control; by this I mean, fishing the holding water that is closest to your side of the river, regardless if you are on the bank or in a boat. Don't make long, unnecessary casts. Position the boat as close as conditions allow, or if possible, cross the river and fish a shorter line.

Fishing the shortest possible line has several advantages to the drift fisherman. The less line out, the less that is in the water, and that means less line drag in the current. Line drag will unnecessarily speed up the drift, giving the terminal rig unnatural speed, even quicker than the present water flow. Any fly fisherman will tell you the same. Fishing a short line means less line stretch. Less stretch means less feel is lost (important with soft-biting fish), and it's easier to drive a hook home without all that line stretch. Here is an experiment for you, to make a point. Take your drift fishing rod and go outside with a friend. Have your friend hold the rod while you take approximately 40 feet of line out. Now, while you hold the end of the line, have your partner "set the hook." Amazing, isn't it, how little force you feel in the end of the line at that distance! Now do it again from 20 feet. There is twice the force with less line out. A short line will also allow for more accurate casts.

In summary, successful positioning is determined by where to stand or anchor at the uppermost section of holding water to begin your presentation; achieving a workable casting distance by getting as close as conditions allow; and keeping as much line out of the water as possible to keep unnatural line drag to a minimum.

2.) The Standard Swing

Once you have determined where to begin your presentation by proper positioning, it's time to cast. One specific drift fishing technique will be used approximately 80% of the year under almost all river conditions, and that is the standard swing presentation.

What angle to cast out will be determined by water depth and speed. You want the terminal rig to be at steelhead eye level by the time it is directly in front of you, not before. For example, if the holding water is swift and deep, your cast will enter the river upstream from your position. If the holding area is shallow, or slow, it may require a cast slightly below your position. This is where on the river experience kicks in. If you are casting either too far upstream or too far downstream to be in immediate control of the drift (remember the workable casting distance), you must make the change on the weight or weighting system to achieve a comfortable drift.

The idea is to allow the terminal gear to get down to the bottom and be presented properly in front of where the first fish would lay. After you have made the weight adjustments for getting the offering down in front of you, it's time to start working the water. You will be casting in a framework, often called fan casting or casting in a grid. This means gradually working out and then down, step by step, from your original position at the top of the holding water. Start with the shortest possible cast and gradually cover the water outward by increasing casting distance with each presentation. The cast will travel or swing downriver at, or

slightly slower than, current speed. This is the ideal drift fishing scenario. The number of casts made in one spot before moving on will always be varied, the number being determined by the actual size of the holding water and degree of visibility. For example, if there is currently 2 feet of visibility, there will be 2 feet between casts working outward. If there is 4 feet of visibility, then 4 feet out, etc. When you have worked the grid in one spot, step downstream or drop your boat downstream and begin a new grid. That is, unless you are hooking one steelhead after another, then by all means stay right there!

How far downstream to begin a new series of casts again depends on the degree of visibility. With 2 feet of visibility, begin

The Standard Swing

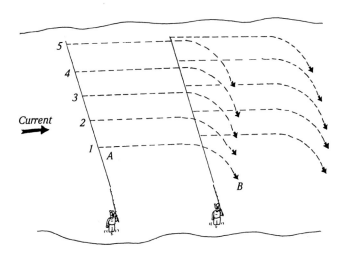

Starting at the top of the holding water, the angler begins working the drift by casting to spot "A" and allowing the terminal gear to travel along with the current until swinging toward shore. (B) The angler will gradually lengthen his casts (1 thru 5) to cover the section of holding water. The number of casts in one position will vary, depending on the size of the holding water and degrees of visibility. For example, two feet of visibility, two feet between casts, etc. When all water has been worked in one position, step downstream to a new position and resume casting, how far to step again depends on visibility—two feet of visibility, step two feet downstream. Casting area is overlapped so no fish will be missed or spooked. Repeat until all holding water is worked.

the new drift 2 feet above where the terminal finished its swing at the end of the last drift. By doing this you will slightly overlap the fan area of the drift, and no fish will be missed or spooked by a line bumped off its blind side.

When your cast is traveling along the bottom, how natural and effective the swing drift will be depends on rod angle and body mechanics. When river fishing, regardless of technique, you always have to deal with certain laws of physics. These laws, when applied to drift fishing, determine that any time the mainline and terminal gear are pulled against the current, the force of the flow will push the gear upwards toward the water's surface and out of the steelhead's range of vision. It is the angler's job to use rod angle and body motion to negate this "push" of water. After the cast is made, the terminal gear settles to the bottom and starts to drift with the current. Here the laws of physics kick in. When the line becomes tight, the bait will start to rise off the bottom. Now the angler must turn his body and follow the drift with the rod. After the angler has followed the drift down, there will be a point where the line is far enough below to again become tight and start to rise off the bottom. Here the fisherman must give line in short, fast lengths to stay in contact with the bottom. If the holding water is short, be prepared to take line onto the reel to keep the terminal gear from settling into the rocks. This again depends on experience and the type of holding water encountered.

It is during the last half of the presentation, or during the swing portion of the cast, that 90% of all steelhead strike the terminal offering. This is because the drift starts to slow at this point, allowing the bait/drift bobber to swing down below the weight, giving the steelhead a chance to follow and take it. Unless there is considerable color in the water (between one and 2-1/2 feet of visibility), make only one or two casts in the same area before making a longer cast or moving down. Steelhead will take a properly presented lure on the first or second drift 95% of the time. Drift fishing is the slowest method of gear fishing for steelhead, and by nature drift bobbers and baits have the smallest attraction radius, therefore you have to present them closer to the steelhead. They do not have the profile or flash of a plug, spoon or spinner, so you must make more casts in a given section of holding water to cover it thoroughly. The only technique that requires more time investment to work a section of holding water is fly fishing. Don't be a "rock lizard" and stand in one section of holding water and make a hundred casts. If no fish come to the bait after methodically working the grid, move on to new water.

At the end of the presentation, there will be a point where the terminal gear has started to slow down, swung into the shallows or is entering non-holding water. Now you must do two things. One, if the water is too slow and shallow to hold a steelhead, immediately raise the rod tip to allow what little current there is to push up the terminal gear out of the rocks, and retrieve the line on the reel to prepare for the next cast. Two, if the section of holding water is deep enough at the end of the swing to possibly hold a fish, leave the bait hanging in the current below for a few seconds. This is an area in which many steelhead are hooked, but most fishermen do not allow them time to take the lure, as the gear is immediately reeled in after the end of the swing. In cold water situations, many lethargic steelhead will follow a bait for many feet before they take. Summer runs in clear, warmer water are notorious chasers. They will come after a bait for many feet after first spotting it, often when it is slowing down in the slower water next to shore.

The ideal position of the rod is with the tip pointed slightly above the spot where the line enters the water. This way, with the rod tip just above the terminal's position, you have leverage to raise the rod and allow the current to pick up the weight, allowing the gear to bounce effortlessly downstream and to set the hook. Always keep the line tight when drift fishing, on that fine line of almost pulling the terminal up off the bottom, yet allowing enough leeway in the line so that it drifts naturally downstream. Inevitably, you will hang up. When you do, try to lift the weight off the bottom immediately. Give it no time to settle into the rocks. Do not yank hard on the rod if the terminal gear momentarily hangs up. A quick lift will allow the terminal to free up and continue drifting. If you yank hard every time the gear hangs up,

you will be pulling the drift lure closer to you, and out of the correct position in the holding water. Jerking hard on the rod will also pull off any or all bait on the hook. A steady, but firm, quick lift is always the correct way to free momentary hangups.

How high or low should the rod be held? Again, this depends on how long a cast is necessary, and how much line is out. As each cast is made progressively longer to cover the water, the rod must be raised higher to keep the mainline out of the water. This keeps line belly (the cause of line drag) to a minimum and is one more reason to fish the shortest line possible. The higher the rod is held, the less "back-strike" area is left to set a hook. We've all done it—had too much line out, and because we had the rod pointed almost straight up to keep the line out of the water, we missed a steelhead because it came off after a few head shakes. Ideal rod angle is anywhere from 9 o'clock (straight out) to 11 o'clock. This variance will allow for enough rod angle pointed up to allow the terminal gear to be worked so it bounces downriver easily, and enough back-strike area left to allow a full hook-setting motion. At all times a relaxed, 10 o'clock position is best for the drift fisherman.

The standard swing presentation is most frequently used as well as the most valuable drift fishing technique. A reminder: no one juggles five running chain saws on the first try. It takes years of practice and a few fingers to get it right. The same goes for steelhead drift fishing. You must take the information and practice it streamside. There are no shortcuts.

3.) The Extended Drift

Sometimes making successive casts to reach water lower in the holding water is not possible. For example, a bank fisherman comes to a steep bank or rock wall that blocks further access to the lower portion of the drift; or a drift boater is working a piece of water near a tricky rapid and does not want to anchor too close to the tailout; or an angler is lazy and doesn't feel like taking a few steps downstream. In these situations, the extended drift will be the method of choice. Often called "freespooling," "tailing," or "long-lining," this technique will come into play during a day's fishing sooner or later.

The extended drift is simply that. When executing the standard swing presentation, at the point where the terminal rigging would start to lift off the bottom, keep feeding line as needed. Instead of allowing the bait to swing into the shallow water on your side of the river, each time the terminal travels downstream and starts to lift off the bottom, give line in short, controlled lengths to stay in contact with the rocks. Repeat this until the holding water is worked as far down as you can keep control of the line. Each time the weight leaves bottom, feed line until bottom is felt; then tighten up the mainline and allow the terminal to travel downstream.

Although the extended drift is a viable technique for covering long stretches of holding water, or covering water that can't be accessed, there is a point where you may have too much line out to control. As we discussed earlier, the more line out, the less feel and control you have. Extend the drift only until you can no longer feel the weight of the terminal rig hitting bottom when freespooling. I have seen many fishermen continue to freespool when their weight was hung up. They were unaware the bait was no longer traveling downstream: they felt only the pressure of the line belly against the current. The advantage of the extended drift is evened out by the increase in rod angle. Remember, to keep line out of the water to avoid drag as your casts become progressively longer, you must raise the rod higher. With the extended drift, to keep feel and control you must hold the rod between the 10 and 12 o'clock positions.

A level-wind reel is tailor-made for extended drifting. Unlike a spinning reel, you can leave the level-wind reel in freespool, and with thumb pressure, allow line to roll off the spool. This is diffi-

The Extended Drift

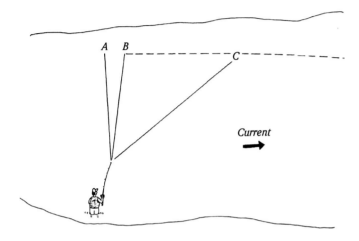

A-B = Start of presentation, depending on current speed

B-C = Normal presentation area of standard swing

 C = Spot where line angle and current will normally cause terminal gear to swing towards shore. This is the spot where line is initially fed to allow gear to keep on travelling downstream through the holding water.

cult to do with a spinning reel, though not impossible. By leaving the anti-reverse switch in the off position, you can back-reel line off the spool to allow for a longer drift. Care must be taken not to reel backwards faster than the line can be taken off the reel, or loops of line will leap off the spool and cause a mess. You have complete control with a level-wind. By using light thumb pressure to feed line in short lengths to stay in bottom contact, you can clamp down on the spool in a split second and set a hook when a steelhead grabs the offering.

The extended drift is a helpful technique, but there is an even more effective way to extend a drift without losing control (see Float Fishing). That will be covered shortly. However, for steelheaders who find themselves unable to reach a portion of holding water they would normally have to pass up, freespooling to increase drift length works fine.

4.) Boondogging and Side-Drifting

These two techniques will be discussed together because they are quite similar. Their beauty is that they take the term "drift fishing" literally. They are both practiced from boats, mostly jet sleds

and drift boats. They are also the easiest techniques for a novice drift fisherman to use, though their simplicity makes them attractive to novice and expert alike. Boondogging and side-drifting are not only simple methods to use and learn, they are also extremely effective on both summer and winter steelhead streams. They are techniques for larger rivers, ones with long stretches of holding water and enough flow that the presence of a boat does not spook steelhead.

I call this method boondogging because it is the term I hear most often by steelheaders when describing this technique. You may have heard it called "boondoggling," or "free-drifting," but they all refer to the same technique. Boondogging is one of the most popular and effective ways to drift fish for steelhead on Washington's larger rivers, with the Cowlitz, Snake, Skykomish, North Fork Lewis, Quilayute and Skagit seeing the most use. The Skagit is presumably where boondogging first came about. Back when the Skagit was used for transportation of logs downstream to the mills, anglers discovered that when a large raft of logs was floated over a long stretch of holding water, the steelhead would bite like crazy.

Boats would then drift behind and along with the logs at 100 feet or so and drag weighted Cherry Bobbers just upstream and behind the boat at current speed. The theory behind this is that when a fish is moved to a new location, it becomes aggressive. Whether the steelheaders of yesteryear were aware of this or not, it certainly mattered little: all they knew was that the floating logs made the fish attack their drift lures.

Boondogging is always done from boats, usually jet sleds and occasionally drift boats, and is used primarily in clearer water conditions, from 3-1/2 feet to unlimited visibility. Because of the speed of the presentation (boondogging is the only drift fishing technique that is done at the same speed as the current, so it is the fastest presented technique), the steelhead need a larger sight radius, not necessarily to spot the bait, but to follow it to strike. In colored water, many a fish will lose a bait before it can turn to take it.

Start by positioning your boat at the top end of a stretch of holding water, approximately 20 feet above the spot you expect the first fish in the run to lay, and approximately twenty feet away, or off to the side of the target water. Allow the boat to free drift with the current. When the boat is parallel to the direction of flow, is traveling the same speed as the river, and is directly across from the very top of the holding water, begin casting. Cast the terminal outfit over to the target water at an upstream angle. A 45 degree angle is about right. Allow the terminal rig to reach bottom; then immediately after bottom is felt, tighten up on the mainline and pull the weight slightly upwards, allowing it to glide downstream with the drifting boat. Because the terminal gear only needs to be in close proximity (within a foot) of the bottom to grab the attention of a steelhead, the weight need touch bottom only every 15 or 20 feet. Doing this will reduce snags and increase feel. Keep the rod at a 10 o'clock position during the presentation.

It is the job of the person running the boat to keep it parallel with the shoreline and steady in the current, either with the oars or a small trolling motor. If there is more than one angler in the boat, the upstream fisherman will cast first; then the person below him casts next, 10 to 15 feet below and either shorter or farther from the spot the first person cast to, and so forth down the line of anglers. Up to four fishermen can boondog if the boat is steady on-line and casts are made in sequence. Because of the freedom that motorized craft and large, open rivers give the steelheader, light gear is often the choice. Longer rods, rated from 4 to 8 pound test and up to 9-1/2 feet, are used to keep line out of the water and

This North Fork Lewis River hatchery summer run was "boondogged" from the jet sled of rodmaker Gary Loomis.

take the shock away from light lines, which average 6 and 8 pound test. Floating along with the river negates the current, and having 100 yards to play a fish in zero current allows the angler to land larger steelhead than you would have thought possible.

Boondogging is done primarily from jet sleds on the largest steelhead rivers. This is because boondogging allows the fishermen

Boondogging

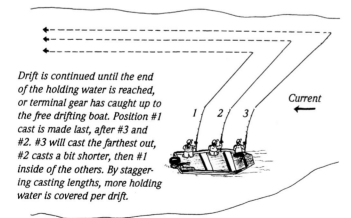

Drift is continued until the end of the holding water is reached, or terminal gear has caught up to the free drifting boat. Position #1 cast is made last, after #3 and #2. #3 will cast the farthest out, #2 casts a bit shorter, then #1 inside of the others. By staggering casting lengths, more holding water is covered per drift.

Jetboat is motored up to the top end of the holding water. The engine is shut off, and with bow perpendicular with the bank, the craft is allowed to drift along with the current. Casts are made by 1 to 4 anglers at a 45° angle upstream and across. Terminal gear will "glide" along, with the weight touching bottom every 10 feet or so.

Boondogging Rig

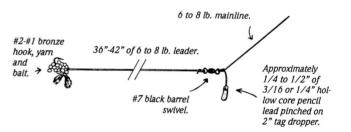

only one drift through a section of holding water. Often this section is up to 100 yards long and half that wide. The jet boater, having a motorized craft, can go back to the top of the run and work a different section of holding water, or the same piece if it is producing fish. Drift boaters do not have that option. Unless the water is slow enough off to the side to be able to row back upstream, they can only boondog one strip of the holding water. On smaller, normal sized rivers, two fishermen boondogging a stretch of holding water can often cover it thoroughly once through. The smaller river more aptly suits drift boaters—without a motor they are limited to one pass. These are the reasons why you rarely see drift boats boondogging on larger rivers and only jet sleds.

Boondogging is simple, easy to teach and done with half the brainwork of the standard swing. It is also very effective, as anyone with access to a jet boat, a large river and a good run of steelhead will attest to that.

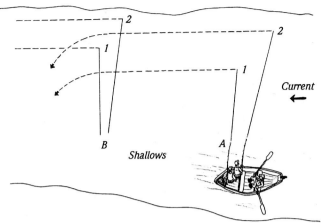

Side-Drifting

Side-drifting differs from boondogging in several important ways. Long-time fishing partner Mike Cronen and I mistakenly called this technique "boondoggin'" for years. Technically what we were doing was not boondogging but "side-drifting." After reading an article on this method in the December/January 1991 issue of *Salmon-Trout-Steelheader* magazine by expert California guide George Burdick, I realized the way Mike and I had been fishing was almost exactly as George described it. George also coined the phrase "side-drifting" in the article, and since this title most accurately describes the technique, side-drifting is what we will call it here. Unlike boondogging, side-drifting is practiced primarily out of a drift boat.

One to two people can side-drift from a drift boat. Unfortunately, the oarsman is stuck rowing to keep the boat steady and moving at the desired pace and doesn't get to fish much. Boat positioning is the same as for boondogging. The oarsman positions the drift boat at the very top and slightly above where the first steelhead may lie in the holding water. Like boondogging, the upstream angler, or the fisherman closest to the holding water casts first, and the second angler casts inside/ouside his cast and below him. The differences from boon-

Side-drifting with guide Herb Jacobsen on the Sol Duc River produced a March native for STS editor Nick Amato.

One to two people can side-drift from a driftboat. With two anglers, each can cover a section of the holding water by making casts of varying lengths. The oarsman positions the boat at the top of the holding water, staying on the oars and dropping the boat down to approximately 1/2 current speed. With the boat travelling at slightly slower than current speed, the presentation will be almost twice as long as the standard swing. When the presentation does start to swing in towards the boat, re-cast back into the holding water, overlapping the presentation area so no fish are missed.

dogging are that instead of casting upstream, casts are made either straight out, or better yet slightly downstream from the boat's position; also instead of a tiny piece of pencil lead the angler will want to use approximately half the weight he would if standing still and fishing the standard swing. While the rower slows the boat down to approximately half current speed, the fishermen in front will cast into the top of the holding water and allow the terminal to drift along much like the standard swing.

With side-drifting, the difference is that due to the length of the drift the fisherman gets, with the boat traveling along at almost the same speed as the river, the presentations will be almost twice as long in length. The cast will still tail out and swing in towards the boat, but it will take longer to finish the cast. When the drift does start to swing in too close to the boat, simply re-cast back into the holding water. The angler is still able to stay within a workable casting distance without having to use the extended drift to achieve the same results. Side-drifting allows anglers to cover a stretch of holding water without having to constantly drop anchor and swing cast. Where it might have taken 20 drifts to work a section of water, side-drifting may cover it in only 5 casts.

The drift boat works well because side-drifting is rarely done along with the river's natural flow. More often it is presented at 3/4 to 1/2 current speed. Where it would be a bit more difficult for a jet boat operator to steer and slowly back down to work the lines, a drift boater can do it with relative ease with oars. Quick adjustments, such as which way to point the bow, and to either drift along faster or slower can be done with a single, swift stroke on the oars. Deeper holes fish better with the boat slightly below the angle of the lines, and shallower drifts are best worked with the lines below the boat.

Side-drifting is the most effective way to work as much water as possible from a drift boat. In a day's fishing, that equals more chances at hookups with steelhead. If you have access to a drift boat, this is the preferred technique on a stretch of open water, void of bank anglers and other boats.

5.) Driftmending

This technique came to me quite by accident. Back in the early 1980s my partner and I were floating a popular stretch of the Skykomish River during the late winter catch and release season. This time of year attracts more than a few fly fishermen. I happened upon two very skillful fly guys who were working the head-in of a large section of holding water. As I watched, I noticed that the amount of time it took for each angler to complete a drift was considerable. The angler would start the presentation by casting slightly downstream and then make as many line mends as necessary to keep the line tight and straight from rod tip to fly. With the rod held at full arm extention, the angler would turn slowly downriver, following the drift of the line and keeping the same tension on it for the entire presentation. By doing this, he fished the holding water at the same speed from the time the cast hit the water until he stripped it in. Then it dawned on me that the reason for the slow, deliberate presentation was the immediate and repeated mending of the line. This eliminated line belly causing the drag that unwantingly speeds up the drift.

Watching them, I wondered if someone had thought of applying this mending technique to drift fishing. The premise was so simple: to mend the line several times at the beginning of the drift to keep the drift speed slow and in control throughout the presentation, not just during the last half of the drift when the terminal starts to slow down on the end of the swing. Oddly enough, not one steelheader I quizzed on this had ever seen it practiced or ever tried it. Naturally, I was curious to find out if the idea was even practical. After experimentation and a modification to the terminal outfit, the weighting system specifically, I found it to

work quite well in many situations/conditions.

To understand driftmending, we must first look at the typical cast and drift with the standard swing. After the cast, which more often than not is slightly upriver from the angler's position, you quickly take up the slack until bottom is felt. Even when it is done to perfection, you don't get total control and feel until the terminal outfit begins to slow down at the start of the swing. As stated earlier, this area is where 90% of all steelhead strikes occur, because the drift has slowed to the point where the fish can reach it easily. Imagine how many more hookups could be had if the entire presentation was as slow and in control as the last half of the standard swing? Here is where driftmending comes into play.

Driftmending is nothing more than an imitation of the downstream quarter cast. To do this and still keep the lure slow and in control, you must use more weight than you would for normal swing casting, up to twice as much (more on this in a moment). Your cast will always be at a downstream angle; how much angle will depend on river depth and current speed. For example, the slower the current, the greater the downstream angle. Leave the reel in freespool or with the bail open so you can give line in quick, short lengths to stay in constant contact with the bottom. Give line, but stay on the reel, keeping all slack out of the mainline. After the cast, hold the rod straight out at the 10 o'clock position, with full arm extention away from the body. From this position, when the terminal gear starts to slip downstream, you can flip the small line belly upriver, mending the mainline like a fly fisherman mends fly line. Reel in the slack between mends, keeping the line straight and tight from rod tip to terminal.

Usually one to three mends will work in all drift fishing situations. By executing these mends, you are not allowing any slack to form a line belly that would speed up the drift. When the line

This trophy Quinault River native hen—all 22 pounds of her—hit a driftmended spinning bobber in a fast, deep run. The author used a two-ounce magnum slinky for a slow presentation.

reaches the point where it starts to lift off the bottom near the end of the swing, turn your upper body slowly downriver and follow the drift with the rod tip. When the drift stops at the end of the swing, reel in slowly; and at the same time raise and lower the terminal gear off the bottom until the lure is back to your position. Many steelhead will follow this "jigged" bait and take it as it is reeled in.

Driftmending keeps the terminal gear at a constant speed, slower than the current, from first contact with the bottom to the tail end of the presentation. To keep the bait at a constant 1/2 to 3/4 current speed, a heavier weight than usual is a necessity. This may mean twice the amount of weight for the conditions. This is the only way to hold the bottom consistently when casting and presenting from this angle. When using this much weight, normally 1/2 ounce or more, rig it so it slides freely on the mainline for feeling steelhead bites more quickly, and not allowing them to feel the weight when they pick up the bait. Fishing slowly like this will take twice the amount of time to cover the water. However, by fishing slower it will double the chances for a hookup, especially in cold water conditions (33 to 40 degrees); when steelhead are lethargic, it may take a slower presented bait for them to reach it. The high rain waters of winter and the snowmelt conditions of early summer are the best conditions for driftmending. High, cloudy or colder water requires a slower presentation. Slowing the bait down like this also works well in fast riffles in the low, clear, warm water (56 to 62 degrees) of summertime conditions.

This technique will ensure that the drift bobber/bait is always downstream of the weight from the very beginning of the drift. With the bait directly downstream, all strikes are felt immediately; the weight doesn't have to travel downriver before a bite is detected. By fishing a constantly tight line, less gear will be lost, because it never gets the chance to settle into the rocks and hang up. The main advantage of driftmending is that instead of being in control of only half the presentation (the area where the terminal would normally start to slow when using the standard swing), you are in control of approximately 80%. You will find that larger steelhead, most notably big males, prefer a slow, deliberate presentation. Driftmending puts you in touch with more steelhead over 15 pounds than any other drift fishing technique.

There are river situations when driftmending is impractical. There will always be one technique that will out-perform another in a given condition. But this one is easy to learn as well as execute, and once you familiarize yourself with it, you will recognize the conditions where its use gives you a needed edge.

Driftmending

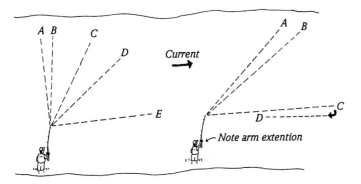

Current

Note arm extention

Standard Swing	**Driftmendingz**
A-B = Initial cast area, depending on current speed.	A = Initial cast.
B-C = No control area, where weight is yet to be felt on bottom, and belly is forming in mainline.	A-B = Line mending area, belly is taken out of mainline, and drift slows to ideal speed.
C-D = Drift slows to ideal presentation speed, belly is taken out of mainline.	B-C = Strike zone.
	C-D = Slow retrieve (jigging) area.
D-E = Strike zone.	

6.) Gliding

When river conditions are cold (33 to 42 degrees), water has limited visibility, or the flow is high and running strong, successful drift fishing requires a technique that keeps the terminal gear moving slowly, such as driftmending or back-bouncing. To fish these slower techniques properly, you must come in frequent contact with the bottom. However, when conditions are fairly clear (4 to 8 feet of visibility) and warm (above 45 degrees), coming in frequent contact with the bottom is not necessary. In these conditions, it can be more of a hindrance to success.

"Gliding" is a technique that presents the bait near the bottom, not on it. In several situations, this will reward you with more hookups. Here is why. When a steelhead is at rest, its eye level will be suspended approximately 8 to 12 inches off the bottom. This, combined with the fact that a steelhead can only see in front and above it, proves that they will have no trouble locating your terminal offering as long as it is presented in close proximity. Plug pullers, spoon/spinner tossers and fly fishermen have proven that a lure glided just above the bottom into the steelhead's cone of vision gets strikes. These techniques rarely, or never touch bottom during a presentation. Why then, do drift fishermen in warmer, fairly clear water have to bang bottom repeatedly during a drift? They don't, and that is where gliding comes in. Gliding is a mid- to warmer-water technique, with the 46 to 62 degree range the best.

To glide your terminal outfit, you must first make a few adjustments. One, use less weight than you would think would be normal for the condition. You only want to come in contact with the bottom infrequently, once to several times maximum depending on the length of the section of holding water and the length of the cast. Two, always choose a slinky as the weighting system. Lead is too jerky, even when it touches bottom once or twice a drift. An exception is if the bottom is fairly smooth. In most cases, a slinky is the best choice for gliding, as it allows for a smooth, natural presentation. A drift bobber is a good addition to the terminal if you are simply using bait or yarn. A drift bobber will help keep the bait suspended and traveling along smoothly.

When gliding, use the standard swing presentation with a slight modification. To keep the terminal outfit coasting along just off the bottom, you must keep constant tension on the line. Any slack will allow the weight, albeit lighter than normal, to sink and bang the rocks too frequently. Once you have cast and feel bottom for the first time, immediately tighten up on the line by slightly raising the rod tip, and if necessary, gathering some line on the reel. This will pull the terminal gear slightly upwards and allow it to go downstream naturally with the current. At the same time, follow the drift downstream with the rod. Don't pull up too much, and don't drop the rod tip unless the gear is traveling into deeper water. After the terminal has traveled 15 feet or so, find bottom again, briefly, and repeat. The weight only needs to touch bottom a few times during the drift to stay within the steelhead's cone of vision.

Gliding has many advantages. It allows you to fish excessively snaggy areas that most steelhead drift fishermen will not risk losing their gear in. By gliding the gear over these areas, you can work lightly fished spots with little chance of hanging up. An uninhibited, current-speed glide is the most effective and natural way to present a drift lure to summer steelhead. Warmer water steelhead have high body metabolism and are therefore hair-trigger spooky. A jerky, irregular presentation may put them down, whereas a smooth, gliding presentation will not. Gliding gives you increased sensitivity, as there are few bottom contacts to deaden the feeling from hook to rod tip. This gives a direct line from fish to fisherman. If you are fishing bait, you will use less during the day. Frequent contact with rocks will pound bait right off the hook, a smooth glide will not. Even if you are not using bait, by drifting above the rocks you will not have to resharpen or replace hooks as often. Sharper hooks, more steelhead.

Remember, in clearer, warmer water conditions, gliding the terminal gear over the rocks will produce more hookups. Incorporate it into the standard swing when conditions allow.

7.) Float Fishing

Float fishing is not true drift fishing, but an entirely different technique. To properly discuss float fishing for steelhead would require another book. Since my personal experience with floats is minimal, and I have only had the opportunity to float fish with a few experts, what you will read in this portion of the chapter will simply be how the float can be used to increase access and opportunities on the river.

Float fishing is a technique our British Columbia neighbors have perfected, as most steelheaders there use floats. They also use much longer rods, and often different reels (see Chapter Six). This is an odd diversity; in Washington and Oregon 90% of the anglers bottom-bounce with drift gear. Which technique is more productive? I can't say, but there are certain river situations where using a float can put the terminal outfit over steelhead where it would be difficult, if not impossible, to do so by bottom-bouncing.

Depending on how heavy your gear is, and how heavy the weighting system is will dictate the size of float you use. Floats between 4 and 8 inches long, and approximately one to 1-1/2 inch in diameter will do the job. Steelhead floats come in a variety of materials: cork, balsa wood and closed-cell foam. Closed cell foam floats are the most popular because of their versatility and inexpensiveness making them attractive to the steelheader. Called "dink" floats by B.C. anglers, they will be the ones that will be focused on in this text whenever floats are mentioned. They are difficult to find in the States, but more companies and private businessmen are now making them available. If you cannot find them, they can be made from the largest diameter backer foam, the same material that the rag drift bobber is made from.

First, let's look at how to rig the float. There are two styles of floats: sliding and non-sliding. For almost all situations, the non-slider will do for occasional duty. Sliding floats require additional pieces to the terminal gear, and are only necessary when fishing water over 10 feet deep. Since 95% of all steelhead lay in holding water shallower than 10 feet, the occasional float user should stick with the non-slider. For the weighting system, rig below the float with the same terminal setup you use when drifting the same conditions. Again, there is a more elaborate weighting system you can use by employing graduations of split shot placed between the float and leader, but for special situation drift fisherman, the standard terminal setup will do. While float fishing this way, you will be using much less weight than when drift fishing the same water. The maximum amount of weight needed is just enough to sink the terminal outfit. Adjust the amount of weight until the float is riding vertically in the water.

When float fishing, adjust the depth so your bait will be approximately one foot from the bottom of the holding water. It is better to start fishing a little deep and shorten the line until bottom is not touched or only touches infrequently. When the float only shudders a few times during the presentation (from touching bottom), you are fishing the float properly.

Foam dink floats have two small diameter, 2 inch long plastic tubes inserted at an angle through each end, from the center of the end coming out the side of the float. This allows the mainline

Rigged Float

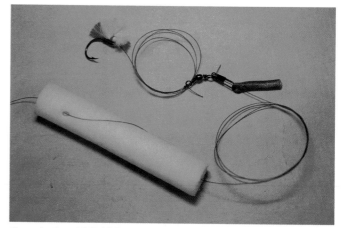

Properly rigged "dink" float, for inaccessible and undriftable water situations.

to be slipped into one tube on one end. By making one wrap around the body of the float and inserting the line into the other tube, the float can be fished non-sliding.

When fishing the float, you will want to keep as much line out of the water (from float to rod tip) as possible. Setting a hook with slack in the line is impossible with a float, and line hanging in the water will unnecessarily speed up the drift. Allow the float to travel at the same speed as the existing current. Strikes are easier to detect than when normal drift fishing. The float is the strike indicator: whenever it moves sideways to the current, upstream, vibrates rapidly, or, more commonly, sharply goes under, it's a steelhead.

Why floats for the drift fisherman? There are five specific situations in which a float allows you to fish water that would be difficult if not impossible to fish with other drift fishing techniques.

In very cold (33 to 38 degree), low-water winter conditions, steelhead often find deep, slow (almost non-moving) pools to hold in. The slow water is the warmest available, and because their metabolism is low and they require so little oxygen, they need only to expend small amounts of energy to hold. At the same time, this type of water can be almost impossible to get a drift in due to the water moving so slowly. A float can provide that drift by suspending the bait. The float eliminates trying to use the tiniest piece of lead or slinky to attempt a drift in the dead water.

In cold water conditions, steelhead also gravitate toward back eddies. A back eddy is a drift fisherman's nightmare—the swirling current pulls the mainline in several directions, making bottom detection after the cast almost impossible until the terminals have settled into the rocks and snagged. Even if the cast is successful, the mainline will surely catch in the current and whisk the bait out of the back eddy shortly thereafter. As long as the mainline from the float is kept out of the current, accomplished by holding the rod high, a float allows the terminal to swirl and dance in the eddy indefinitely, or at least long enough for a fish to find the bait.

You may come upon a situation where the river bottom is covered with unforgiving tree branches, clay ledges or obnoxious boulders. While gliding your offering over these nasty spots may be the answer, there are occasions when any gear allowed to bounce—even once—on the bottom will be snagged and lost. The float, set at a safe distance of approximately one foot above the snags, will allow you a drift through a spot other steelheaders have passed up. As long as the water temperature is above 43 degrees, steelhead will be active enough to move aggressively out of the obstructions and come the short distance for the bait.

Awkward positioning is the major call for floats. As discussed earlier, positioning is the most important part of any drift fishing technique. Sometimes bank anglers find themselves too far below or above the holding water, all access blocked by natural obstructions. If the angler is below the holding water, he can use a float to make a natural presentation. The float will suspend the terminal and bring the bait back down to the angler's position without having the current speed up the drift unnaturally, or the weight being wedged into the rocks at this abnormal angle. If the angler is too far above the holding water so that an extended drift is impractical, the float will do the same thing: present the bait at the same depth and speed no matter how far away the float may be from the angler. By freespooling and keeping the mainline out of the water to avoid drag, a properly presented extended drift is possible where it would not be without the float. Feel is not a factor. As long as you can see the float, that will be the tip-off to any strikes. Keep line stretch in mind when long-lining a float like this; it is almost impossible (remember the test with your friend?) to set a hook when a steelhead is over 50 feet from your position.

Keep a few dink floats, or other types of medium-sized, non-sliding floats in your vest to be able to fish effectively in these situations.

Nick Amato used a float to get a drift in the cold (34 degree) slow flowing water in the background to trick this Michigan steelhead.

8.) Plunking and Back-Bouncing: The High Water Solutions

In Chapter Two, we discussed finding steelhead by water temperature and degrees of visibility. We saw how high, off-colored water conditions make 95% of the river too fast for steelhead to rest in. The only areas slow enough for fish to rest in are usually next to the bank, near the lower end of the holding water near a former tail-out. Steelhead will search out these areas because they are the only spots slow enough to rest in; they also have the least amount of suspended silt. In this high, dark water there will be a parting, or transition line where fast water meets slow. Within a foot of this line to the bank is where steelhead will lay. Due to severely limited visibility, from 2 inches to one foot, normal drift fishing techniques do not work. Plunking and back bouncing, however, are tailor-made for these conditions.

It is during these water conditions that steelhead move. The higher water allows for easy passage over obstructions, and the dark water is excellent cover. However, now that you have moving fish and limited visibility, you also have a problem. A moving lure, even a slow moving one, is impractical because the fish are traveling up, the lure is traveling down, and there is virtually no visibility. A hookup would be a miracle, or you need a large number of steelhead to increase the odds. When steelhead move upriver, they follow the contours of the banks along the transition lines. Your best bet under these circumstances is to place the lure/bait in a fixed position directly in front of steelhead traveling upstream. This is plunking.

A special setup of the terminal outfit is necessary for plunking. Bait is almost always used; the added scent and profile aids the steelhead in finding the lure in the poor visibility. There are many scents on the market that may be applied to any or all parts of the plunking rig to aid steelhead in the darker water (see Chapter Five, Scents). Because of limited visibility, the largest and brightest drift bobbers with the most action should be used. Plunking calls for winged bobbers: the #4, or larger #2 Spin-N-Glow are the top choice, the #2 Flashing Spinning Cheater next, and then the #5 Birdie. All spinning drift bobbers used for plunking should have one of two color schemes, either glow-in-the-dark (the best) or chartreuse. The large drift bobber keeps the bait and hook suspended at the proper height above the bottom. Remember, steelhead will sit and travel just above the bottom—from a foot to 20 inches above it. Therefore, you have to place the bait at 18 to 20 inches off the bottom.

Tie the large, bright, spinning drift bobber, hook and bait to an 18 inch leader of 12 to 20 pound test. In this limited visibility, steelhead cannot see piano wire, so line diameter is not a factor in hooking fish. Attach the leader to a three-way swivel. Do not use the cheap brass "T" shaped ones; they bend and break easily under pressure. Make these three-way swivels yourself. Start with a #6 split ring and three #5 crane barrel-type swivels, and put the swivels on the split ring. This makes a flexible, strong three-way swivel with zero weak points. Unlike commercial three-ways, these allow total freedom of movement and a direct pull from fish to mainline. Tie the 15 to 20 pound test mainline onto one of the swivels, the leader and terminal onto the swivel next to it. On the remaining one, tie 20 inches of 10 pound test dropper line to a pyramid-style lead weight. The lighter 10 pound dropper will allow you to break off the lead and save the remaining terminal outfit if it becomes snagged. The pyramid-styled sinker grabs bottom and holds its position in the current better than any form of lead. Three to 6 ounces should suffice to hold bottom, depending on current strength.

Once a plunkable spot has been determined near the transition line, from your position carefully place the setup in the water so that mainline, leader and dropper do not become tangled. Slowly lower the setup until bottom is reached. Allow the setup to sit out at no greater an angle than 45 degrees, or you will lose the advantage of the dropper. When the weight stops firmly in the desired spot, place

Plunking Rig

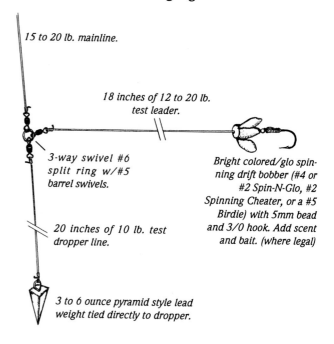

15 to 20 lb. mainline.

18 inches of 12 to 20 lb. test leader.

3-way swivel #6 split ring w/#5 barrel swivels.

Bright colored/glo spinning drift bobber (#4 or #2 Spin-N-Glo, #2 Spinning Cheater, or a #5 Birdie) with 5mm bead and 3/0 hook. Add scent and bait. (where legal)

20 inches of 10 lb. test dropper line.

3 to 6 ounce pyramid style lead weight tied directly to dropper.

the rod in a rod holder (or good old forked plunking stick) and tighten up the line until the sinker is just about to be raised off the bottom. This creates a tight, straight line from weight to rod tip. Doing this will ensure that the lure is working freely away from the mainline, and if a steelhead should wake you up and strike, it will be on a tight line.

Plunking should not be restricted to high, off-colored conditions. Many anglers prefer this method in lower stretches of rivers where steelhead are only moving through and not holding. By toning down size and color of spinning drift bobbers and by using smaller baits, you can plunk for steelhead in these lower reaches anytime the water has adequate flow and color for them to move upriver.

When rivers have that teasing color, from 12 to 18 inches of visibility, there is still not enough light penetration for normal drift fishing techniques, yet there is enough visibility that plunking is only one solution. In the upper stretches of rivers where steelhead are holding, you can use a modification of drift fishing; such as back-bouncing. This is not true back-bouncing, like that done from the back of a boat when fishing for spring Chinook, but the concept is the same, so that is how we will refer to it here.

In this dark water you still need the combination of action, size (profile), color and smell to attract steelhead. The more senses you trigger, the greater your chance the fish will find the lure. For the back-bouncing rig, start with a large, spinning drift bobber, like a #5 Birdie, #4 Spin-N-Glo or #2 Flashing Spinning Cheater. Stick with the same colors you would use for plunking, due to severely limited visibility. Glow-in-the-dark, chartreuse, white or black are the best choices. When there is so little light penetration that even chartreuse is ineffective, glow-in-the-dark will still carry light and attraction down to the steelhead. Use a 5mm glow bead between the hook and the drift bobber, and contrasting yarn in the bait loop. Add the proper size bait and scents to the drift bobber/yarn. The smell of baits/scents will emit a cone of scent that gradually spreads out downstream. This will literally stretch the attraction radius to several feet below the terminal gear, alerting steelhead to its presence and perhaps triggering a sense of anticipation.

Run the spinning bobber/hook/bait onto 18 inches of 12 to 20 pound test leader. Tie the leader to a #5 crane style barrel swivel, and the 15 to 20 pound test mainline to the other end of the swivel. Remember, water conditions are high, and the river is running strong. You will need heavier gear to control and land a powerful steelhead. They cannot see the heavy leader, so it will not be a factor in getting strikes. Leave a 4 inch dropper tag on the mainline after the knot is tied to the swivel. From this dropper, you can attach a small #10 snap swivel for a magnum slinky, bell sinker or pinch on 1/4 inch diameter pencil lead, depending on the makeup of the river bottom. Now we are ready to back-bounce.

The trick is to fish this heavy terminal outfit as slow as possible, yet still get a drift. Because of the off-colored water, you will be fishing between 2 and 4 feet deep. Steelhead will stay fairly shallow, because there is less silt in shallower water, and it will be a degree or so warmer. Start at the uppermost section of the holding water (the spot where the transition line first forms and the area becomes flat) and lower the terminal into the river. Long cast are rare in high, off-colored conditions; holding water is normally close to an angler's position, near his feet. Begin the presentation by allowing the rig to sit in one spot on the edge of the parting line, and allow the big, bright, smelly lure to work for 3 to 5 seconds. Now lift the rod and bounce the terminal backwards allowing the offering to slip straight downstream approximately a foot. How far downstream is directly related to degree of visibility. For example, in 8 inches of visibility, move the rig downstream 8 inches, and so forth. Do this the entire length of the holding water. When finished, go back to the top of the holding water and start over either one foot farther out or closer to the bank.

Normally, steelhead will simply stop this rig, not striking hard but rather with a surprisingly soft mouthing. Back-bouncing is always done on a short line, so all bites are felt easily and immediately. Under conditions of severely limited visibility, the river will be a lonely place, with the majority of anglers at home waiting for clearer flows for normal drift fishing. By plunking and back-bouncing, steelhead can be hooked in marginal conditions.

When drift fishing for steelhead—winter and summer—you may be surprised by other anadromous fish picking up your bait, such as: (top left) chum salmon, (bottom left) sea-run cutthroat, (top right) Dolly Varden, (bottom right) pink salmon.

CHAPTER 5

NATURAL STEELHEAD BAITS

Say what you will about the endless debate over whether steelhead actually feed once they enter fresh water. While it is truly up in the air if winter steelhead feed, summer steelhead—especially those freshly arrived from saltwater, as well as those in late fall just before winter holdover—do actively feed if the opportunity presents itself. It is also a fact that steelhead, regardless of the time of year, geographic location, strain of fish, or water clarity and temperature will take a natural bait. When drift fishing, it is not necessary to use bait; steelhead can be tricked to take solo drift bobbers, yarn, or a combination of the two. However, it has been proven by countless anglers over many decades that bait added to a drift bobber or bait fished solo will draw strikes 10 to one over an artificial drift lure. Theories vary as to why this is so; it could be the smell of the bait, it could be the sight of it, or it could be a latent feeding instinct left over from the ocean or when the steelhead was a juvenile in the river. We will never know exactly why steelhead take a bait; we only know they do, and this is why drift fishermen rely so much on natural baits.

Natural baits give the drift fisherman a few advantages. One, a steelhead will hang onto a drift lure longer if there is bait adorning the hook. Where they would only grab and quickly reject a hard-bodied drift bobber, a steelhead will give a bait a few more chews before rejecting the offering. These few extra chomps give the angler a precious second or so grace period to feel the bite and set the hook. Two, baits will work in any water condition, from high and off-colored to low and gin clear. In high, limited visibility conditions, natural baits put out a cone of scent, alerting steelhead of the bait coming its way, even when it cannot yet see it. In unlimited visibility conditions, a natural bait will trick even the most scrutinous fish into biting, for no artificial bait on the market looks or smells like the real thing. There are many steelheading techniques that cannot make this claim, or that must be changed dramatically to adapt to conditions. Not so when bait fishing.

There are a few general rules to follow when using baits. Like drift bobbers, the size of the bait should match conditions: for example, in low, clear conditions, use a small bait that closely matches, or is slightly larger than, the appropriate drift bob-

This 14 lb. Puyallup River steelhead decided a gob of chum salmon eggs was too good to pass up.

ber. In higher water, increase the profile of the bait so the steelhead can find it. When placing the bait on the hook, it is important to always leave the tine of the hook exposed. This guarantees that no part of the bait can block the hook point from finding the steelhead's mouth. Nowhere is there evidence, even in glass clear water conditions, that an exposed hook tine keeps steelhead from biting. A buried hook can impede a hookset, especially on a light bite, or if the fish is over 30 feet from you and line stretch is a factor. The take on bait ranges from a subtle stop to an arm-yanking rip. The way steelhead take baits directly relates to water temperature. In cold water (33 to 42 degrees), expect a deliberate mouthing, or a simple halting of the drift. In warmer water, when fish metabolism is higher and they are more aggressive, takes on bait can still be subtle, but expect a swift, hard yank 90% of the time.

Which bait has the greatest attraction to steelhead? Nine out of ten anglers will say roe, and they are probably correct. However, keep this in mind. A study done in 1989 by West Coast biologists on captive steelhead throws a curve to the roe theory. For one month steelhead were fed every known bait. The one they never spit out and took under all varying temperatures and lighting was...the marachino cherry. Right. The same ones you find floating in a cocktail glass. Hmmm. Unusual baits (like the cherry) won't be discussed here. There is either not enough information available to properly describe how to fish them, or they are not effective on steelhead. For example, there are several commercial dough-baits sold by large companies that claim amazing results. The truth is, they have a yam potato base (the kind you eat on Thanksgiving) that is effective only on planted hatchery trout, and their appeal to steelhead is minimal.

Effective as baits are on steelhead, they are not always legal to use. There are river systems that change regulations at specific times, and some rivers have year-round bait bans. Before using baits, carefully check the regulations for your state or province to see which baits are legal. The following covers the most popular baits for steelhead.

1.) Salmon/Steelhead Roe

It's not known who the first person to hook a steelhead by drift fishing was, but you can bet that fish bit a gob of roe. The original steelhead drift fishermen in the early 1900s were exclusively egg tossers. Drifting roe and fly fishing were the first methods known for taking steelhead. Out of all the dozens of lures and techniques developed since then, drifting roe is still the most effective method in all conditions for attracting steelhead. Roe can be obtained from either salmon (Chinook, coho, chum, sockeye or pink) or hatchery steelhead that have not yet become "ripe" (meaning that their egg skeins are still tight and have not separated).

Which species of salmon (or steelhead) produce the best eggs for steelheading is a matter of preference. Chinook eggs are the largest; not only in quantity from an obviously larger fish, but each individual egg is much larger than other salmon eggs. For this reason the Chinook is highly valued for its roe. The coho and the sockeye have eggs that are normally bright red in color, while chum and pink eggs are light orange to light pink; steelhead eggs are light orange to light yellow.

Individual egg size varies between salmon. The usual breakdown is this: Chinook have the largest eggs, followed by chum

and coho, then steelhead, with sockeye and pink the smallest. I have not found one type of roe that will outfish another if both are cured and presented properly, nor have I seen evidence from anyone else to prove one is superior to the other. One thing to remember: take eggs only from hatchery steelhead! A native fish is too valuable to kill for its roe.

To illustrate the uncanny effectiveness that roe has on steelhead, consider the following. As you may know, the legendary Skeena River and its famous tributaries support the largest steelhead on earth. The Babine River is one of the most popular tributaries, and every September and October hundreds of the best spoon, spinner, drift and fly fishermen converge there. In years of good water conditions and large numbers of fish, the number of hookups per day with any of the artificial lures mentioned above (roe and all other natural baits are banned year-round on the Babine) is approximately 6 steelhead on the fly, 15 on drift bobbers and 20 on spoons—exceptional numbers. When the river's lodges shut down operations at season's end near the first part of November, Bob Hooton, Regional Fisheries Biologist for the British Columbia Fish and Wildlife Service, and two others employ a jet sled. Then they methodically fish each pool, from the weir at the end of Babine Lake (the origin of the river) to 10 miles downriver. Their purpose is to tag steelhead and see how many fish are in the river. They fish roe solo on drift gear. In a typical day, the three will *land* over 100 steelhead between them, in the same water that was pummeled by lure and fly tossers. Any questions on the effectiveness of roe?

Roe is fished in small chunks called "clusters." When the roe is cured, pieces of clustered eggs are cut off the skein. Depending on water conditions, use smaller clusters in low, clear water, to larger clusters in high, off-colored water- the clusters will range from the size of your thumbnail (on a #2 hook) up to the size of a 50 cent piece (on a #3/0 hook). For most river conditions and hook sizes, the roe cluster will be the size of a quarter. When placing the cluster on the hook, push the point of the hook through the bottom half of the cluster until the hook tine is exposed. Open up the egg loop, slide the cluster up the hook shank and place the other half of the cluster in the loop; then snug it down until it is just tight enough to hold the eggs onto the hook, no tighter. Always use the bumper, or egg loop tie, for attaching leader to hooks when fishing eggs; the loop of line on the hook is what secures the eggs during the rigors of casting and drifting.

Roe

Two examples of properly rigged roe.

Unless you use a cure that makes the cluster as tough as rubber, roe will always be a delicate bait. Always cast with a deliberate motion when fishing roe, as a wrist-snapping action will fling the bait off the hook. A soft, lobbing cast is the choice when fishing eggs. Because of their delicate nature, egg clusters cannot take repeated pounding off the rocks without breaking and washing out. Around three casts is the life expectancy of an egg cluster, sometimes more depending on the distance of the cast and bottom structure. You can prolong the drift life of a cluster if you do not abruptly jerk the rod each time the terminal gear stops. A deliberate, short, firm lift will allow the weight to continue its drift without pulling the roe off the hook. In any case, after the cluster is milked out, when the eggs have popped and all that is left is the white membrane, replace it with a fresh cluster.

Favorite Rig

The author's favorite low-water bait: small cluster of borax-cured salmon roe, pink yarn, a #14 black drift bobber and #1 hook.

If cluster eggs are not available, single eggs may be bagged up into simulated clusters by using soft, fine maline mesh cloth available at most sporting goods stores. The maline comes with no-knot thread that sticks to itself. After twisting the eggs into the cloth by bringing the four corners together, make 3 or 4 wraps with the thread and pull until it snaps. Trim off the excess maline flush with the thread. Use 4 to 8 single eggs in the cloth, and you will have nifty little clusters that last somewhat longer than plain roe. (See photo.)

Roe Bags

Ingredients for "roe bags," from the left: tiny cluster of eggs, maline cloth and no-knot thread. The finished roe bag (right) is placed on a #2 hook with yarn.

Be aware that some rivers and areas have roe bans prohibiting the use of eggs, also be aware of the presence of smolts (baby steelhead) when using roe. Smolts are always actively feeding while maturing in their home rivers and are extremely aggressive toward roe. They will rip a good cluster off a hook in seconds, not unlike a school of piranha stripping flesh off some luckless animal careless enough to wade into the water. Smolts will often take eggs deeply, along with your hook, and this can result in smolt mortality. Smolts are a common nuisance in spring months when they are migrating downriver toward sea. When smolts are present, use an artificial lure, drift bobber or yarn, or a larger, tougher bait they cannot strip off the hook or fit into their mouths.

When using drift bobbers in tandem with clusters, it is common pratice to use a round drift bobber when visibility ranges from gin clear to 2-1/2 feet. The Corkie and Okie Drifter are the best match for roe; the sizes you use will be matched to conditions. Try to keep drift bobber/roe cluster size similar. Too big a chunk of roe, matched with too small a drift bobber, will nullify the neutral buoyancy provided by the bobber. Roe is a heavy, dense bait and needs a similar sized drift bobber to support it off the bottom. If you are using a large cluster and a tiny drift bobber, it is better to substitute the bobber for yarn, as the drift bobber's function has been demoted to attractor. In reality, any of the styles of drift bobbers will work. The theory behind using the round drift bobber over other shapes is that the eggs and the clusters themselves are round, thus increasing the attraction factor by simulating additional roe, or simply not alerting the steelhead to something of unnatural shape hanging onto the eggs. Regardless of whether you use them with a drift bobber or solo, a cluster of roe is the best and most versatile steelhead bait.

Curing and Storing Roe

If you are lucky enough to get mature, prime salmon/hatchery steelhead skeins, you must learn how to prepare them for curing, as well as how to store them. There is one rule to follow when curing eggs: never, EVER freeze fresh, uncured skeined eggs. Freezing discolors them. More importantly, when uncured eggs freeze, they develop hairline cracks. You cannot see the cracks and the eggs will appear to be fine to the touch, but when you cast them out and they hit water, all the juice in the eggs will run out like a popped balloon. Repeat: do not freeze eggs until they are cured. There are dozens of egg cures, both home-made and commercial. All will attract steelhead, some better than others. It is how the angler presents the roe that determines which cure works best. Here are some of the most popular home-style recipes for curing roe clusters.

Borax Cures

In the glory days of steelhead fishing in the 1950s, the rivers that emptied into Puget Sound had the most plentiful runs of winter steelhead (along with large numbers of summer steelhead) found anywhere. This was the era before chemicals were used to preserve eggs. Then, all a steelheader had was powdered borax to toughen up the roe so they would last longer. From the Puyallup to the Skagit, all steelheaders cured their eggs in borax. Their

catch statistics were astronomical, and today many an old-timer will swear loyalty to the cluster rolled in borax. Boraxed eggs are still the most popular today and in my view remain the undisputed champion over any other egg cure seen or tried.

To cure and store eggs in borax, you need enough 99% Mule Team Borax (do NOT use hand-soap borax, it is too gritty and has added perfume scents) to cover all the eggs you are going to put up, usually one box per 10 medium-sized skeins. Also, you will need a pair of scissors, paper towels, a mixing bowl, newspapers, and enough metal, glass or plastic containers to hold them all. Avoid styrofoam containers. When packed full, they generate heat which will excessively dry out and burn the eggs, making them useless. Not a very nice surprise when you get to the river and open a styrofoam container with the day's egg supply hard as clustered marbles.

Start by taking the fresh, skeined eggs from the fish. Wrap them in a layer of paper towels and set them in the refrigerator for a few hours to remove all the excess water from the egg skein. Your working surface will be a few layers of newspaper covered with a layer of paper towel, creating a surface large enough to hold all the eggs you plan to cure. Unwrap the skeins and cut them into bait-sized chunks or clusters. Set the clusters on the paper towel approximately 3 inches apart, and allow them to air dry until they become tacky. Timing is important. Do not let them dry too long, and don't go to the next step if they are still slippery wet.

After one side of the egg clusters becomes tacky, turn them over onto the dry space between clusters where there is no egg juice. Let this side also become tacky. Now, in a separate bowl— we'll call this the mixing bowl—pour some 99% borax. Then take two or three clusters at a time and drop them into the mixing bowl. Shake the bowl enough to work the borax into the nooks and crannies of the egg clusters to absorb all the juice that may be left. When the clusters are sufficiently dusted with borax, they are ready to go into containers for storage. Be sure to dump out the borax in the mixing bowl when it starts to get lumpy and turn color; the clusters must be rolled in clean, fresh borax to absorb the excess juice.

Take more fresh borax (not the used borax from the mixing bowl) and pour an even, thin layer on the bottom of the storage container. Set the borax-covered clusters evenly in the container, side by side. When a layer of egg clusters is done, cover with just enough fresh borax until you no longer see them. Repeat until there are enough layers of egg clusters and borax to fill the container. Top off the container with fresh borax and seal. Allow the egg clusters some curing time by placing them in the refrigerator for 2 to 3 days. Then freeze them. They will last for years once frozen, and can be frozen and thawed several times and still stay in good shape.

This is the oldest recipe for curing eggs. Borax cured eggs look, feel and smell like fresh roe. The only thing borax does to eggs is toughen the membrane holding them together, so they

will stand up longer to the rigors of casting and bouncing off rocks. The borax toughens only the membrane and leaves the natural juices inside the egg. Steelhead will hold onto boraxed eggs longer than any other cure. Where a fish will simply pick up "chewier" cured eggs and immediately reject them, they will chomp on the boraxed roe cluster until it is gone. This is a tremendous advantage to the reaction time afforded a steelheader.

Here are some variations to the borax cure. Lay the skeins on the newspapers and paper towels. Split the skeins down the middle, butterfly style, and let air dry until tacky. In a small bowl, mix equal parts of white granulated sugar (not powdered) and plain non-iodized salt. Sprinkle the mixture on both sides of the skein to the point of almost covering the eggs. Place in the refrigerator overnight on fresh paper towels to allow most of the juice to run off the skein. The next day, cut into bait-sized pieces, roll in borax as before and put in containers.

For these next two variations, you will be soaking the eggs in a solution. Take the butterflied skeins and soak them in a solution of one quart water, one-half cup salt and one-half cup brown sugar for approximately one hour. Take the skeins out and allow to air dry until tacky; then cut into clusters and borax them as usual. Or, you can use a solution of one quart water, one cup salt, one cup brown sugar, and one cup 99% powdered borax. Mix all ingredients well in a large plastic container. Cut the roe into clusters, then place them in the solution for 10 to 15 minutes. Pour the eggs and solution into a pasta strainer and set the clusters on newspaper and paper towels until tacky on both sides. Roll in borax and store as before. For added color, some anglers mix equal parts of raspberry or cherry Jell-O to the above mixtures, or sprinkle it on after the eggs are taken out of the solutions.

Borax cures are the least messy of all egg cures. Unlike other cures that rely heavily on dyes or leave eggs in a sticky/tacky state that makes them feel as if they were covered in honey, borax-cured roe is dry to the touch, and only the powdery borax itself sticks to your hands. The major drawback of eggs cured in borax or sodium sulfite is all the goop left on your hands after digging out a cluster and securing it to the hook. A quick rinse of the hands in the river (not fun in cold weather) or a wipe on the small, handy towel hanging off your vest will remedy this.

Sodium Sulfite Cures

Not as popular or as easy to use as borax cures, sodium sulfite nonetheless makes eggs tough and durable and is preferred by many steelheaders over borax formulas. It is sodium sulfite you want to buy, not sulfate or sulfide. Drug stores and photographic supply houses carry sodium sulfite. Sulfite cures eggs in a constant tacky-sticky state, with the consistency of a "gummi bear." They last longer than borax-cured eggs, though steelhead tend to just mouth these eggs before spitting them out. They will not hang onto them as long. Here are some sodium sulfite cures.

Start by cutting fresh skeined roe into bait-sized clusters. Set them on several layers of newspaper covered by a layer of paper towel. Mix up equal parts of granulated white sugar, non-iodized salt and sodium sulfite. Sprinkle the clusters with the mixture, just enough to lightly cover them. Turn them over and do the other side. Take the clusters and set them (one layer deep only) into a glass or aluminum oven pan deep enough to contain the juice, and refrigerate overnight. The next day, drain off the juice and put the roe into containers. You can roll them in borax to make them less messy to handle, or use them as is. They will last indefinitely if frozen and up to 8 months in the refrigerator.

A variation with sodium sulfite starts by butterfly-splitting the skeins and placing them skin-side (membrane) up on the newspaper/paper towels. Lightly sprinkle the split skeins with even parts sodium sulfite and cherry or raspberry Jell-O. (Jell-O adds color and helps preserve the eggs.) Place the skeins, as before, in shallow pans for approximately 2 hours, and allow the juice to drain off. Cut into cluster baits, or put whole into containers. After 2 to 3 days in the refrigerator, they may be frozen and will keep indefinitely.

If one of these home-made cures does not appeal to you, or you don't have time, there are commercially available roe cures that will do the job quickly and easily. These premixed formulas are easy to apply and will cure/color eggs with satisfying results. The following cures are available in a wide market at almost any sporting goods outlet:

Pro Cure Egg Cure
Pro Cure Products
P.O. Box 13699
Salem, Ore. 97309
1-800-776-2873

Pro Glow Egg Cure
Beau Mac Enterprises
1802 37th Way S.E.
Auburn, Wash. 98002
(206) 939-8607

Siberian Bait Cure
Siberian Salmon Egg Co.
Arlington, Wash. 98223
(206) 435-0313

Oregon Egg Cure
The Guide Shop
12140 Hwy. 6
Tillamook, Ore. 97141
1-800-243-4746

Mr. Shur-Cure
(West Coast)
P.O. Box 903
Tillamook, Ore. 97141
(503) 842-2565

Mr. Shur-Cure
(Great Lakes)
Jim's Bait Service
319 E. 14th St.
Duluth, Minn. 55811
(218) 722-1279

Alaska Borax Formula Bait Cure
Alaska Premier Bait
6900 191st Place N.E.
Arlington, Wash. 98223
(206) 435-6600

Quick-Cure
Shell Marc International
P.O. Box 8000-312
Abbotsford, B.C., Canada V2S-6H1
(604) 852-4575

If not using roe straight out of storage containers, be sure they are carried on the river in a non-collapsible container. Eggs allowed to jostle and get squashed will not have the same appeal to steelhead and be a mess to handle. A hard plastic, inexpensive bait container (the style that slips onto a belt and is secured to the waist) is ideal for bank fishing with roe. No matter which roe cure you choose, home-made or commercial, borax or sodium sulfite, mark all containers with the date they were cured. Use the oldest eggs first so you always have good looking roe that appeals to steelhead.

2.) Shrimp

Since the early 1970s, shrimp has been jousting with roe for top billing as a steelhead bait. There are many followers in the

Sand (Ghost) Shrimp

Sand shrimp properly rigged (left): with spinning drift bobber for limited visibility conditions and for the "crawling" illusion, and (right) with narrow drift bobber for clearer, warmer water conditions.

shrimp's corner who in many circumstances claim they will out-fish eggs. It makes sense to use shrimp as a steelhead bait, because it's their main diet in the ocean. We will be focusing on two types of shrimp for steelhead: the sand or ghost shrimp and the deep water shrimp, or prawn.

The sand shrimp lives in a mud/sand area in the lower tidal zone. Sand shrimp range in size from 2 inches long to almost 8; most sand shrimp for steelhead baits will be 3 to 5 inches long. The sand shrimp ranges in color from a rather drab off white/light yellow to a brilliant array of magenta, bright orange, yellow, red and purple. These multicolored shrimp are better and smaller baits on the average than drab-colored ones. Both sport dual claws, one larger than the other, both capable of inflicting a painful nip when handled alive. Make a point to twist off the pinchers before fishing, as steelhead will take a declawed sand shrimp quicker than one sporting claws.

Always use sand shrimp that are alive or freshly dead. They are such a delicate bait that after they have been dead for a few hours, they become mushy and less appealing to fish. Do not attempt to freeze sand shrimp. Being made up almost entirely of water, they split and become mushy if frozen. Keep them cool when fishing in warm weather. Use them alive and fresh, or as a last resort, purchase dyed and preserved sand shrimp. Cured sand shrimp are a poor substitute for live, fresh shrimp.

When rigging the sand shrimp, if using them in tandem with a drift bobber, there are a few tips to remember. Round bobbers are recommended for roe because they closely resemble the bait. When fishing sand shrimp, the choice of bobber enhances the performance of the bait. In water conditions that are at or slightly below moderate levels, are somewhat warm (47 to 60 degrees), and have good visibility (from 3-1/2 feet to clear), use an elongated, low-action drift bobber: the #1 Pill or Cheater in sizes #10 and #12. The theory behind the elongated drift bobber is that its slim profile matches the shrimp, squid or krill that steelhead feed on in the ocean. When water conditions are colder (35 to 45 degrees), switch to a spinning drift bobber with sand shrimp to excite steelhead.

Moving lethargic fish to take the shrimp is not the only reason to switch to a spinning drift bobber. It's the author's opinion, one shared by many veteran anglers, that a spinning drift bobber is the best style to use when fishing with sand shrimp in any water temperature or stage of clarity. When fished at a slow spin, the rotating wings give the illusion of the shrimp actually crawling or swimming with its front legs. It is for this reason the sug-

gestion is strongly made to fish spinning drift bobbers with sand shrimp. Be careful to match the size of sand shrimp (as you would a drift bobber) to the conditions. The rule to remember is the clearer and warmer the water, the smaller the shrimp. In high, low visibility or colder water conditions, use a larger shrimp for increased profile; in lower, clear water conditions, if smaller shrimp (3 to 4 inches long) are not available, simply pinch off the head and use the tail section only. Most outlets that sell live sand shrimp normally sell them by the dozen in large and small sizes.

Bait Threader

Bait threaders are helpful in keeping delicate sand shrimp on the hook.

Sand shrimp are the most delicate and fragile steelhead bait. However, there are ways to rig the shrimp that prolong its casting and drifting life. Treat the sand shrimp like a cluster of roe when casting. Slower, deliberate motions instead of a swift, wrist-snapping cast will deprive the steelhead of a free lunch of sand shrimp that has just been flung off the hook. Always place the shrimp "upside down" on the hook, with the tail up next to the drift bobber and the head hanging down. The hook point should be inserted just below the tail and the hook threaded through the body. Place the egg loop of the leader around the fan of the tail to hold the shrimp on the hook. As when drifting roe, avoid jerking the rod each time the terminal stops (unless it's a steelhead), as this will pull the delicate shrimp off the hook. With small 3 to 4 inch shrimp, the standard drift bobber/hook-to-conditions matchup will suffice for holding bait on. There are several commercially available bait threaders that allow you to slide the sand shrimp up onto the line where it will stay on longer. Position the hook at the end of the bait so the steelhead will always be grabbing hook first, insuring a solid hookup nearly every time. (See photos for proper riggings for sand shrimp.)

When using light terminal gear (6 pound test with #2 hooks, for example) you will not be able to use a larger hook to hold the long body of a sand shrimp properly. Using only one small hook, even on the smaller shrimp, will result in more lost bait and missed strikes. A double-hook or tandem rig will hold the shrimp on best and makes for a can't miss dual-hook setup that results in a 95% of bites-to-hookup ratio. Start with two #1's, two #2's, or a #1 on top and a #2 on the trailer hook. Tie the hooks as you would a saltwater salmon mooching rig for herring (using the bumper or egg loop tie), approximately 2 to 2-1/2 inches apart. When putting on the sand shrimp, place the top hook above the tail in the first segment of the body. Slip the egg loop over the fan of the tail. Place a yarn tie into the loop to keep the line from cutting through the shrimp. Insert the trailer hook into the head, or as close to it as possible depending on the length of the shrimp body.

Double Rig

This double-hook rig will hold sand shrimp more securely, and is a "can't miss" setup when a steelhead sucks in the bait.

Sand shrimp are the most effective bait under four specific conditions. First, you can use shrimp as an alternative bait on popular stretches of holding water on rivers that receive a lot of pressure. Observe what other anglers use; if they are drifting roe or plain drift bobbers, use shrimp as an alternative to what the steelhead are accustomed to. Switching to shrimp will often result in hookups on busy rivers. Second, use sand shrimp in cold water conditions (33 to 42 degrees). Steelhead, especially hatchery fish, seem to prefer sand shrimp over other natural baits in prolonged cold water conditions. Third, use sand shrimp in high, off-colored water. They give off more scent than any other natural bait. This added smell aids steelhead in finding the bait even when they can't see it. And due to their basically hollow body, shrimp are tailor-made scent holders. (See "Scents" later in this chapter.) Finally, the sand shrimp is a superior bait near tidewater sections of winter rivers. Winter steelhead that are hours out of saltwater take sand shrimp aggressively, possibly due to a latent feeding response from recently eating shrimp out in the sea. Regardless of why, they will take a sand shrimp eagerly in the tidewater sections of rivers.

Prawns

Properly rigged prawns with a spinning (right) and a round drift bobber for high and normal conditions.

Called the prawn or deep-water shrimp, these cousins of the sand shrimp are equally effective on steelhead. Hardly a new bait, deep-water shrimp have been used to tempt Atlantic salmon in Great Britain since the mid 1800s. It wasn't until approximately 1960 that the prawn was first documented for steelhead drift fishing in the Northwest. Prawns have been around for a decade longer and are fished differently from the sand shrimp: they are used without their heads; they are used in different river situations; and unlike sand shrimp, these shrimp have action.

Prawns are an inexpensive, durable bait. A pound of deep water shrimp will cost approximately five dollars. A pound gives you around 30 baits. When buying prawns from the seafood section, avoid the prawns with bodies over 3 inches long. Being a fatter-bodied bait than the sand shrimp, any prawn with a body over 3 inches long becomes too thick for a hook smaller than a #3/0. Prawns over 3 inches need to be segmented, or broken up into two or three separate baits. The prawn is thicker through the body than the sand shrimp and is a dense, firm-bodied bait. Visually, they are a better bait if left whole bodied.

With prawns there are two ways to fish them: either fresh (raw) or cooked. When fresh (uncooked), they are a drab gray in color and have rather soft shells that do not need to be removed before fishing. Uncooked prawns give off a natural and increased amount of scent than when cooked. When purchased pre-cooked, or when dropped in boiling water for 3 minutes, the shrimp will turn a bright orange and their shells will become hard. The cooking process removes a lot of the natural scent. These hard-shelled shrimp need to be peeled before use, or a steelhead will quickly reject them. There are some types of deep-water shrimp, however, that have rather soft shells even when cooked and should be fished unpeeled to prolong the drift life of the bait. All deep-water shrimp have short legs which should be left on for added attraction. Which ones to choose, either fresh (raw) or cooked, depends entirely on angler preference. Cooked prawns will keep longer and are a bit more durable. Each catches fish equally well.

When hooking up the prawn, I have seen it done two ways, but only one fishes well. Start by removing the head if the prawn is sold with head attached. A pinch and a twist will do. Unless the prawn is very small (2 inches long or less), always remove the head, as it interferes with proper rigging and adds excess profile to the bait. Next, remove the tail in the same fashion. The tail should be removed, as tails are hard and sharp and add extra unnecessary profile to the bait. The shrimp body will be thick at the head and tapered toward the tail. The thick head of the shrimp should be positioned up on the hook near the drift bobber. Prawns have a permanent crescent curve in their bodies. The hook should be placed on the inside of the body where the small legs are. Insert the hook point a half-inch below the head of the body, on the inside curve of the prawn. Thread the hook into the body until the hook tine is exposed. The hook should be almost hidden in the body of the shrimp. Now slip the egg loop of the leader over the half-inch head of the prawn to secure it to the hook. This is the proper way to hook deep water shrimp for drift fishing, with the head positioned up. By hooking it in this position, when drifted against the current, action will be imparted to the bait, making the shrimp spin in a tight roll. This spinning action, combined with sight and scent, gives the drift fisherman a bait like no other. When hooked with the head down, on the other hand, the shrimp will only roll slowly in the current. There will be too much body obstructing the hook point, interfering with a proper hookset, and too little meat near the tail to insert into the egg loop to hold it on the hook.

Prawns are effective with any style drift bobber, but the spinning style is the best choice. As when using the spinning bobber with sand shrimp, they give the illusion of the shrimp crawling or swimming. This has great appeal to steelhead, especially in colder water or limited visibility situations. Deep water shrimp, the cooked variety in particular, are a durable bait. They can take the pounding from rocks and repeated casts without losing their shape, color or appeal. A prawns durability allows you to make longer casts without fear of snapping off the bait on the release. They can be fished for dozens of presentations or until a steelhead strips it off. This longevity makes the prawn desirable over other baits in several river situations. First, when walking or floating miles of river, it makes sense to probe the holding water with a few pieces of inexpensive, durable bait rather than wasting valuable fishing time constantly rebaiting hard to obtain softer baits (like roe and sand shrimp) when looking for concentrations of steelhead. The prawn is the ultimate searching bait for this reason. Second, the prawn is the best natural bait when there is a high concentration of smolts. A baby steelhead can whack and chew on these larger, tougher baits all day with little chance of swallowing them. There is almost zero smolt mortality when using prawns.

Searching Rig

Prawns are excellent in high water, as their tough bodies will absorb a lot of abuse (they won't fall off) and not lose appeal to steelhead. Because of their toughness, they make a good "searching" bait.

Properly rigged, a dozen cooked or raw deep-water shrimp will last an entire day, unless the fish are really biting! Prawns are effective in water conditions that are high with limited visibility (12 inches to 3 feet), to conditions that have at least a tinge of color (4 feet of visibility). They may be stored frozen up to a year in plastic containers, and if they are kept cool, unused shrimp may be refrozen a half dozen times and not lose color, scent or shape. Prawns are a low-maintenance bait: they can simply be put into a plastic sandwich baggie and stuffed into a vest pocket. (See photo of properly rigged deep water shrimp)

3.) The Best of the Rest

Roe and shrimp aside, there are nearly a dozen additional baits that appeal to steelhead. These will be included here because there will be times and conditions when these baits will be alternatives to the common denominator of baits used by the drift fishing majority. They may work even better than roe or shrimp under rare occasions; they may also be easier to obtain in certain locations and may be pressed into emergency duty when there is no other bait available. All the baits we will discuss here are proven steelhead attractors.

Worms (Nightcrawlers)

Call them what you want—dew worms, nightcrawlers or leaf worms—they are a great steelhead bait. My first encounter with a summer steelhead (purely accidental) was while trout fishing one October in the upper reaches of Washington's Carbon River. After hooking several bull trout (Dolly Varden) up to 18 inches in one particularly sweet stretch, my worm was intercepted by something much larger, more colorful and powerful than anything I had ever hooked there. The beautifully colored native summer run, which I estimate now at 10 pounds, made my tiny spinning reel and ultralight rod buck and screetch. Only for ten seconds, however, as my 2 pound test mainline was severely overmatched. It didn't help matters to simply stand there paralyzed with mouth agape as the fish jumped and snapped the line. Worms work!

Since that day, many steelhead, winter and summer, have been duped into taking a worm. Along with the shrimp, the worm probably triggers a latent feeding response from the smolt stage in the river, where freshets would wash worms into the water. Summer steelhead, especially since many are actively feeding, will aggressively take a worm. Worms are easy to obtain and almost any outlet that sells bait will have a supply of lively worms, either 3 to 5 inches, or "nightcrawler" from 5 to 9 inches. These larger worms are the ones to use for drift fishing. Digging your own worms can be easy and fun if you look in damp, loamy soil. Store worms in the refrigerator if bought commercially in styrofoam containers, or, if you dig them, store them in a cool, dark place in the same soil they came from. Keep them in large coffee cans, or better yet in old planter boxes. Always use lively, active worms. Dead worms do not have the same action on the end of a hook, nor the proper scent.

Rigging the worm for drift fishing is simple, but care must be taken not to kill the worm immediately. Insert the hook point half an inch below the head of the worm and thread the hook through the center of the body up the shank of the hook. Leave the hook tine completely out of the body and secure the egg loop around the head of the worm. This will allow 75% of the nightcrawler to dangle and wriggle seductively. You may think that leaving this much worm dangling invites a fish to rip off the trailer and miss the hook. Not the case. When a steelhead takes a worm, it will take the entire bait or none at all. Worms for steelhead bait have two major drawbacks. First, there is the chance smolts will take the worm and hook deeply. This is the main reason for using larger worms for steelhead. The best choice during late spring/early summer is not to use worms when smolts are present in large numbers. Second, a steelhead (a summer run especially) will take a worm deeply 8 out of 10 times. This means options for releasing that fish have been reduced, for swallowed baits can result in a bleeding fish. If you are fishing in rivers with the majority of the run of hatchery origin and you plan to keep one for the table, go ahead and use worms.

As with sand shrimp, use an elongated drift bobber that compliments the long, thin profile of the worm. The #1 Pill is the ideal bobber for low, warmer, clear water; and a small spinning drift bobber like the #14 and #12 Spin-N-Glo, the #10 Flashing Spinning Cheater, and the #0 Birdy gives the crawling illusion to the worm. The worm is effective in the full range of water temperatures and degrees of visibility from glass clear to 3 feet. Any less visibility than 3 feet and the worm, due to its subtle brownish color, will not be readily seen by steelhead. Keep in mind that nightcrawlers are a somewhat delicate bait, and a deliberate, smooth cast is required so they are not snapped off the hook. Worms will last a half-dozen casts or more before breaking in two, or are no longer wiggling.

Steelhead take worms with an aggressive, deliberate grab, with no subtle mouthing that you may get with roe. Carrying the worms on the river can be a nuisance but worth the extra effort. Place them in a cooler if the weather is warm, and keep them out of direct sun when walking river banks. Put them in a noncollapsible container with tiny air holes poked in the top. Worms not used and still lively can be placed back in the cool storage place at home or back onto the lawn.

Nightcrawlers

Properly rigged nightcrawlers: set on the line and hook with a bait threader (right), and with a narrow drift bobber (left).

Crayfish

Called crayfish, crawfish or crawdads, these relatives of the lobster are wonderful steelhead baits. An extremely popular bait in southwest Washington for summer steelhead, crayfish will work at any time of the year, in any water temperature or degrees of visibility. Tiny crayfish (1-1/2 to 2 inches long) may be fished whole, rigged as you would a small sand shrimp. However, crayfish tails are normally the only part of the creature used. The most common way to fish them is to break the head off and discard it, leaving only the tail. Depending on the size of the crayfish, each tail has several segments which contain white, fibrous meat. Peel off the shell. Each segment is broken into separate baits and placed on the hook in the same way a roe cluster is fastened. (Most crayfish I have used, even larger ones, have enough meat in the tail for one bait only if you are using a hook larger than a #1.) Crawfish meat works with any style drift bobber that is matched to the conditions.

Live crayfish are preferred, as the meat is somewhat more durable when fresh. Fresh crayfish (raw) is oily, and gives off a lot of scent in the water. You can boil the tails for approximately 3 minutes to make the meat tougher, but cooking the tails takes all the oils out of the meat and some scent will be lost. Uncooked crayfish meat is a drab gray, cooking turns it bright white. Most anglers prefer to use it uncooked, as it is plenty durable raw. Tails can be purchased at almost any fish market, and live crayfish can be bought at selected bait shops. If you know of a stream with a population of crawfish, there are commercially available traps that will get your bait for free. Tails can be frozen indefinitely, but once thawed need to be used the same day, as they spoil rapidly.

Crayfish are a good choice for bait during spring when there are large numbers of smolts present, or the crayfish are molting (shedding) their shells. This leaves them with a vulnerable soft shell for a few days, and opportunistic steelhead will take advantage. Being a tough bait, they can be carried in a small plastic bag in the shells until broken apart and set on the hook.

Crayfish

Crayfish tail (left) and properly rigged crayfish meat.

Squid Tentacles

Here is a bait you probably haven't come across but is one I have seen steelhead take readily. Squid is the most obvious choice for a steelhead bait, because it is what a steelhead feeds on in the ocean. The entire squid, however, is much too large to use for a drift fishing bait. Here, only the tentacles are used and then only 2 to 2-1/2 inches.

There are two ways to obtain squid tentacles. First, if you are lucky enough to live in the Puget Sound region, you may jig for them at night during winter months off one of many public piers.

Rigging for Squid Tentacles

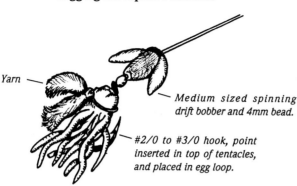

Yarn

Medium sized spinning drift bobber and 4mm bead.

#2/0 to #3/0 hook, point inserted in top of tentacles, and placed in egg loop.

The other option is to go to any large seafood market. Purchase whole squid only. To make baits, cut off the tentacles just below the eyes, so they stay attached to one another. If the tentacles are over 2-1/2 inches long, trim them down to this length with a sharp knife. Be sure to eat the other portions of the squid, as they are delicious. Do not cook the tentacles, they are plenty tough as is, and cooking them will remove much of the natural scent.

To rig the squid tentacles, insert the hook point into the center of the "top" of the tentacles (where they come together near the former head) and place the egg loop over it, allowing the tentacles to hang down. The choice of drift bobber will always be the spinning style, as they mimic perfectly the undulating motions a squid body makes as it swims. Squid tentacles are a good choice in water with limited visibility (12 inches to 3 feet). Because of their larger profile, they are best used in higher water conditions. Being such a tough bait, they can be cast without anxiety of the bait flinging off, and can be used when there are high concentration of smolts. Best of all, no one else on the river will be using squid, so on heavily fished water this gives the angler a novel alternative bait. Squid can be frozen, or rolled in borax like roe, and stored. Their toughness makes carrying them on the river simple. Place enough tentacles for a day's fishing in a small plastic bag.

Granted, this is the hardest bait to obtain, as squid is seasonal. I have had some difficulty finding them at any time other than January, February or March. In late winter, I've found that large native steelhead will chase down and hammer this bait like a lure. It is the only bait known to take steelhead in salt water, at the only well-known saltwater fishery on Whidbey Island's Bush Point in northern Puget Sound.

Grasshoppers

Grasshoppers have seasonal and geographic limitations to their effectiveness. However, when used at the right place and time, can produce steelhead strikes when nothing else will. In eastern Washington and Oregon, there are half a dozen summer run steelhead streams that receive the majority of their fish in late summer and early autumn. At this time, there are hordes of grasshoppers in the tall, dry grasses that border riverbanks. Large trout, especially steelhead, have become conditioned to these insects landing on the water and will feed on them. The Klickitat, Grande Ronde and John Day rivers are several of the best rivers

Winter steelhead are deeper-bodied than their summer kin, because their body cavities are filled with mature roe and milt. This egg-heavy March hen shows off her girth.

where grasshoppers produce.

Rigging the grasshopper is simple. Thread one, two or three of them onto the hook by inserting the hook point under the head, allowing them to sit on the bend of the hook. Small drift bobbers work best with grasshoppers, as they are the only natural bait that is somewhat buoyant. The #14 Corkie or #14 Cheater work fine, as the additional buoyancy of a larger bobber is not needed with grasshoppers. A better choice than a drift bobber would be one or two colors of yarn for contrast.

Grasshoppers are a tough, durable bait. The only problem is catching them. An aquarium net of approximately 8 inches in diameter aids in trapping the elusive insects. A fly swatter is also popular. Ones not used for bait at the end of the day may be released, as grasshoppers do not keep in captivity (read bait box) for very long before expiring. The real trick is to remove one or two of the 'hoppers from the bait container without releasing all the inmates.

Caddisfly Larvae ("Periwinkles")

Also a seasonal bait, larvae of the caddisfly will sometimes get steelhead to bite when normal baits fail. They are effective in low, clear, warmer water periods when summer steelhead go into nonbiting doldrums. "Periwinkles," as they are more commonly known, are a delicate bait found clinging to, or under, stream rocks. They build a casing around themselves of sand and twigs, which give them camouflage. They are abundant in all clean running steelhead rivers from late spring through summer. For summer steelhead, caddis larvae are effective baits. Personal observations of stomach contents of dozens of summer steelhead have sometimes revealed bellies full of the dark casings of caddis larvae. One Oregon summer run had mistaken a black pen cap for a caddis larvae case!

To rig caddisfly baits, gently separate the casing from the larvae by breaking the casing in half, carefully so as not to destroy the larvae inside. Use the largest ones you can find. Gently insert the hook point just under the spot where the black head meets the soft, yellow body. Thread 4 to 6 of them onto the shank. Use small hooks with periwinkles, sizes #4 and #2 in fine wire, as they are a delicate bait and a larger hook will split them. Use without a drift bobber, as you will be fishing the caddisfly larvae in the warmest, clearest conditions of the year. Very little color or profile will be necessary. Adding a small tuft of black yarn can enhance the bait, however.

There are two major drawbacks to the use of caddis larvae. First, they attract trout better than steelhead. Most of the trout you hook during the summer months are steelhead smolts; they will take the larvae deeply, especially with small hooks. Use your best judgment when smolts are present. Secondly, they are a very delicate bait and cannot withstand more than a few drifts. They must be cast with a deliberate, smooth motion. Larvae need clean, flowing river water to live, so take from the river only the amount you expect to use immediately. The best situation to use the periwinkle in is if you have spotted a steelhead that has refused all other offerings. Gather some caddisfly larvae out of the shallows close by and try them for a few casts.

Maggots

Unlike caddisfly larvae, the larvae of the common horsefly is a durable insect and twice as disgusting to look at. So effective are maggots on trout that they are banned for use in most of Europe. Maggots have an appeal to steelhead. Simply ask some of the mid-winter whitefish anglers that have had their mornings made (or ruined!) by the unexpected steelhead tearing up their ultralight gear. Maggots are no longer than 1/2 to 3/4 of an inch long, so they are fished in the same manner as the caddis larvae: 4 to 6 of them threaded onto the shank of a #2 or #4 fine wire hook. A hardy bait, especially when hooked just below the tough skin of the "head," the maggot will stay alive and wriggle seductively for *hours* on the hook. They work best in low, clear conditions, winter or summer. Most outlets that sell live bait also carry maggots. Storing and carrying them on the river is as easy as putting them in a small container with corn meal and keeping them cool. Maggots will live for approximately one week. As with caddis larvae, smolts take maggots deeply, so use good judgment if smolts are present.

Have we forgotten to mention your favorite bait? No matter. If you have a preferred bait not mentioned here, and you have complete confidence cast after cast that it will draw steelhead bites, don't change. However, when legal, adding bait to a drift bobber or bait solo will favorably increase the chances for a hookup. Just don't leave for the river without some marichino cherries...

Periwinkles (caddis) Grasshoppers and Maggots

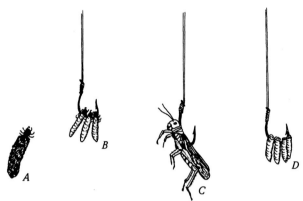

A = Caddisfly larvae in it's shell.

B = Properly hooked caddis on a #4 or #2 hook, just under their hard, cartridge-like black heads.

C = Grasshopper with #2 hook placed just under it's hard "collar" behind the head. Grasshoppers carefully hooked in this manner will stay alive for several casts.

D = Properly hooked maggots. Maggots have extremely tough skin immediately behind their "heads," and hooked up on a #4 hook they will stay alive for many casts.

4.) Scents

First used by the steelhead drift fishermen in the mid-1970s as several bait oils, today's commercial scents are available in liquids and pastes, with dozens of added scents and colors to increase the appeal of drift lure or bait to the sea-run rainbow. While adding scents to baits or lures is more important in salmon fishing than steelheading, there are several advantages and river conditions in which adding scents to bait/drift bobbers will increase chances for hookups.

The first advantage of adding a scent is to mask any undesirable odors the lure/bait may have picked up. Humans give off a chemical called L-serene that alarms salmonids. Adding a scent to a bait is a good idea for no other reason than to mask undesirable smells. The second advantage is it helps stimulate another of the steelhead's senses, making them more prone to bite. There are two river situations/conditions where stimulating the fish's olfactory sense will increase the chance for a hookup. In cold (33 to 42 degree), clear water conditions, steelhead will be lethargic, and a bait with added scent seems to work much better than the natural scent of the bait alone. However, where the addition of scent to bait makes a significant difference is when rivers are running with limited degrees of visibility.

When visibility is limited (12 inches to 2 feet), light penetrates weakly and not very deep. That is why large, bright drift bobbers with action make the most out of what little light is available. When plunking or back-bouncing, adding scent to the bait will increase the attraction radius two-fold. Scents released from the baits will disperse downstream below the terminal gear, creating a cone of scent, widening gradually as it disperses below the lure. Unlike other components of the drift gear—the drift bobber, the bait, etc.—the scent will alert steelhead of the presence of the bait long before it sees it. This will create anticipation and guide the steelhead to home in

Scents

These commercially available scents help steelhead find baits/drift lures in cloudy water and help trigger strikes from cold water, lethargic fish.

toward the origin of the scent, possibly triggering aggressiveness from the fish. The fact is, scents play an important role in high, low-visibility conditions.

There are two forms of scent used by steelheaders: solid form, in paste or gels, and liquid oils. The trick with scents is making them last and not wash off after one presentation. To make the scents last you must choose one form of scent, and decide what to apply it to. For hard-surfaced lures like drift bobbers, use a gel- or paste-bodied scent that will stick and not wash off. Paste will release scent into the water for approximately half an hour before having to be reapplied. No need to glob on paste or gel scents; just smear a thin layer over the drift bobber. For baits, you may also smear on a thin layer of paste scent, but injecting all baits with scent oils is the best way. (There are commercially available bait injectors. See photo.) When simply sprayed or squirted on a bait, oils will wash off quickly. When injected into baits, oils will seep out slowly, leaving a scent trail in the water below the bait. Scent oils will last ten times longer when injected into the bait versus applying them to the outside. Yarn, because of its absorbent nature, will accept either paste or liquid scents.

Which scent is the most effective? Every drift fisherman has a

Bait Injector

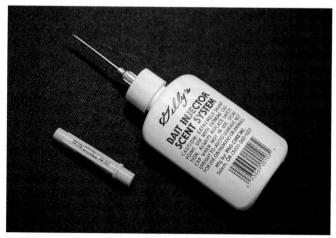

Bait injectors allow you to put scent oils into the baits instead of on the outside. Injectors make scents last ten times longer.

favorite. Even human saliva is supposed to attract steelhead. The problem in naming the most productive scent is that *all* of the commercially available scents attract steelhead. I have heard testimony from dozens of excellent drift fishermen on their favorite scents. Some swear to anise oil, some to shrimp oils, some to garlic. So how do you choose? The best way is to match the scent to the bait. For roe, choose a salmon egg oil or anise (licorice) oil. The author's first summer steelhead picked up "licorice eggs" after dozens of other steelhead refused plain boraxed eggs. Inject the roe by inserting the tip of the injector needle into the center of the cluster. Eggs cannot take much oil injected into them, a few drops will do. If you are using smaller clusters and injecting them is too time consuming or otherwise impractical, dip the cluster along with the yarn into the oils, or spread a light coating of the same in paste form on the cluster.

Injecting oils is the choice for both sand shrimp and prawns. Sand shrimp are basically hollow creatures and accept scents better than any other bait. Use a sand shrimp oil (make sure it is a sand shrimp oil and not just plain shrimp) or herring oil. Insert the injector needle into the body of the shrimp. Fill the body cavity with oil, at the same time slowly withdrawing the needle from the shrimp. For prawns, use a shrimp oil or herring oil. Insert the needle into the prawn, and while slowly withdrawing the needle, squirt a few drops of oil into the shrimp body.

For nightcrawlers, the best choice is a worm oil. If that's not available, use a sand shrimp oil or anise oil. Worms accept injected oils well; inject them the same way you would a sand shrimp. Insert the needle into the body of the worm and withdraw slowly while injecting a few drops of oil. Crayfish and squid tentacles have no storage area for injected oils, so they are better fished with gels or paste scents. For crayfish, smear a light coating of real crayfish paste, or shrimp paste if not available. For squid, use a squid paste on the tentacles, or anise based paste.

For other baits, the situations they are fished in do not require an added scent, or they do not accept scents well enough to bother. Experimentation is the key with scents, the only boundaries being your creativity. Don't be shy with re-applications. If you believe the bait/drift bobber/yarn needs more scent, it probably does.

There are many commercially available scents you can experiment with: sardine, anchovy, herring, squid, garlic, even WD-40. You can buy the previously mentioned scents in oils and gels/paste, and many combinations of flavors. Here is a list of commercial scent manufacturers:

Pro Cure Products
(13 different bait oils, 12 different bait pastes, bait injectors)
P.O. Box 13699
Salem, Ore. 97309
1-800-776-2873

Siberian Fish Attracter Oils
(8 different bait oils)
Siberian Salmon Egg Company
6900-191st Place N.E.
Arlington, Wash. 98223
(206)-435-0313

Atlas-Mike's Bait Company
(7 different bait oils)
P.O. Box 608
Fort Atkinson, Wis. 53538

Smelly Jelly
(11 different gel scents)
Catcher Company
Hillsboro, Ore. 97124
(503)-648-2643

When legal to use, natural baits and scents add another dimension to your steelhead drift fishing. Which baits will work the best for you can only be determined by experience. When you can recognize water conditions/situations that determine roe over shrimp, shrimp over worms, etc, then natural baits will consistently help you increase steelhead strikes.

CHAPTER 6

THE TOOLS—RODS, REELS, LINES AND OTHER PERSONAL GEAR

Almost as important as reading water, your drift fishing gear must match up with situations, conditions and your quarry, the steelhead. In this chapter we will discuss which oufits will best suit terminal riggings and techniques. There will be no mention of brand name rods, reels, or lines, for each angler has a favorite brand, style or combination that feels "dialed in." Secondly, where you are steelheading has a significant influence on the selection of a drift fishing oufit. Simply compare the rods and reels used by anglers in British Columbia, the Northwest and the Great Lakes. For these reasons, we will only look at outfits that make drift fishing the easiest and most effective for current river conditions and techniques.

In Chapter Six, we will be discussing tools for steelhead drift fishing—rods, reels, monofilament lines, how to set up a vest and how to choose waders and other personal gear.

1) Rods: The Important Match

Matching the rod to river conditions is the number one concern for river anglers. The material the rod blank is made of does not enter into the puzzle, because each fisherman has their own idea of which is right for them. Even though steelheaders should lean towards lighter, stronger rods to avoid fatigue and increase sensitivity, there are still many who prefer the old fiberglass. So the argument of high modules composites versus graphite, graphite vs. glass, is not necessary. While one weight of rod blank may be a favorite to the individual steelheader, there will be situations where a lighter, or heavier, weighted rod will be more effective. In his classic book *The*

Steelhead Trout, author Trey Combs states this clearly: "A ten pound steelhead may be found at tidewater or in violent canyon rapids, in rivers that ocean tankers negotiate, or tributary creeks several rod lengths wide. No one outfit can be expected to answer all these needs."

Steelhead rods range in length from 7-1/2 to 12 feet long, but for most practical drift fishing purposes rods will be 8, 8-1/2 or 9 feet long, with the most popular length being 8-1/2 feet. Rods in these three lengths are long enough to keep line out of the water to avoid line belly, short enough to maneuver easily and light enough to avoid wrist fatigue. Drift fishing rods are rated by their action, which describes how and where in the blank the rod will flex. There are fast, medium and slow action rods. Fast action means the greatest amount of flex is in the top quarter of the blank; medium action means the blank flexes in the top half; and in a slow action rod the blank flexes uniformly through the top three-quarters. These actions determine how heavy a weight and pound-test line will match, as well as how much sensitivity and power (in terms of setting the hook and playing steelhead) the rod has.

The author made the right choice in rod, reel and mainline to tame this Vancouver Island summer run.

Rods

All commercially manufactured rods have a suggested line weight/lure weight on this portion of the blank.

Choose a rod that has the correct number of guides. One of the easiest rules to follow when buying a rod is one guide for each foot of rod. An 8-1/2 foot rod should have no fewer than 9 guides, counting the tip. The rod fights the steelhead, not the line. When there are too few guides, the line will follow the rod contour unevenly, causing stress points on the line. There must be enough guides so that the line follows the bend of the rod as closely as possible. This is most important with lighter lines.

Today's rods are built with guides that protect the line from abrasion. Unlike the plain metal guides from yesteryear that would eventually wear a groove and cause line damage, these guides can take years of constant use and show zero wear. These guides are made in three grades: ceramic (the least expensive), hardaloy and SIC, which are the slickest (the least amount of friction) as well as highest quality.

Today's drift rods are either made for level wind, spinning or center-pin reels. Except for British Columbia steelheaders, the center-pin reels are scarce in the States, and so are the rods for their use. I have not fished with one, and though I've had the pleasure of fishing with dozens of expert steelheaders, none of them unfortunately were knowlegeable about this Canadian method. Canadian float rods are 10 to 15 feet long, the length is necessary to keep the mainline out of the water to prevent drag during a presentation. These rods have a specially designed handle accommodating the center-pin reel (a handle that is not easily found commercially in the Northwest).

The rods you will find commonly used for drift fishing for level-winds and spinning reels have certain features to look for. I highly recommend any model with a trigger handle for a level-wind rod. The triggers themselves are usually built in direct contact with the rod blank, adding extra feel. On cold days, the trigger allows for an easier grip on the rod. Also, playing fish (and unfortunately, breaking off when snagged) is done without having to squeeze the rod. Both spinning rods and level-wind rods have a 12 to 14 inch butt section behind the reel seat. This long butt balances the rod. Most anglers tuck the rod butt under the forearm

The early summer run—affectionately called the "springer"—is the most sought after steelhead. "Springers" jump high, strike hard, and fight fiercely.

Now you are fishing the typical steelheading scenario: a medium sized river, water is slightly above normal flow and the water is a perfect green tint with 3 feet of visibility. To match this condition (there is a lot of leeway) you choose a 12 pound mainline, a 10 pound test leader and a #1/0 hook. A rod with an 8 to 12, or 8 to 15 line rating will be the choice. This is a medium-action rod with the flex in the upper half of the blank. Rods of 8 to 12 or 8 to 15 are the most popular with steelhead drift fishermen because they cover the greatest number of lines that can be used, from 8, 10, 12, 14 and 15 pound tests. Medium-action rods have enough flex to protect lighter lines like 8 and 10 pound test, yet have enough backbone to set a larger hook like a #2/0 or #3/0. With medium-action rods, you must match the hook size to the pound test of the mainline. A rod of 8 to 10 or 8 to 15 can handle weights of 1/2 to 3/4 of an ounce without over-flexing. Any weight heavier than 3/4 ounce will stress the blank and may cause damage to the rod. Rods weighted 8 to 12 or 8 to 15 are ideal for most drift fishing situations, winter and summer, and will accommodate the widest choice of line tests and weighting systems.

Then there are the power rods, the ones used when you're after trophy sized steelhead; when fishing large rivers; or in high, off-color water conditions. Twelve to 20 pound test mainlines, with 10 to 15 pound leaders, are the norm. For these situations, you will want to choose the heaviest practical steelhead rods weighted from 10 to 20 pound test. These are fast action rods, with the flex in the top quarter of the blank. Fast action rods have enough power to set a larger hook, like a #2/0 or a #3/0, with ease and help control larger steelhead or fish that are using the heavy current as leverage. A rod rated for 10 to 20 can handle weights up to 1-1/2 to 2 ounces, which equate to large pieces of pencil lead, magnum slinkies or small bell sinkers. All high water and trophy steelhead drift fishing should be done with a 10 to 20 weight rod. The only drawback with fast action heavy rods is when you're casting for accuracy and distance. Without at least half the blank flexing when loading up to cast, you must exaggerate the casting motion by turning your body more than usual in order to transfer enough power to achieve the distance. This extra motion can lead to fatigue after many hours of casting.

Plunking rods are the heaviest rods used for steelhead fishing. Because of the heavy weights used to hold the terminal gear fixed on the bottom, the rod must be able to support weights up to 6 ounces when casting and not over-flex. You may want to substitute a salmon mooching rod for the job, one with a 15 to 25 or 15 to 30 pound test rating.

Ideally, the drift fisherman should keep three different rods for matching varying river conditions: an 8-1/2 to 9 foot 6 to 10 (light, slow action), an 8 to 9 foot 8 to 12 (medium action), and an 8-1/2 to 9 foot 10 to 20 (heavy, fast action). These three rods are the most popular and common on Northwest steelhead rivers, as they will cover any situation and make a good foundation for the drifter's rod collection.

while making a presentation. This extra leverage allows for more powerful hooksets and less wrist fatigue while playing fish.

All commercially made steelhead rods and blanks have a recommended line and lure weight printed immediately above the front cork grip. This rating tells you which rod will work in varying drift fishing situations. Let's look at some examples.

You are fishing low, clear conditions. To match this condition, you choose an 8 pound test mainline, and a 6 pound leader with a #2 hook. A rod with a 6 to 10 pound test rating will be the choice. This rod will be a slow action rod with a lot of flex, which will protect the light line from shock. This extra flex will allow you to use delicate baits, as the rod is slower to load up when casting, therefore less likely to snap off the bait when trying for distance. A rod of 6 to 10 pound line rating can handle weights of 1/4 to 1/2 ounce without over-flexing the blank, losing accuracy on casts and control during a presentation. Any weight heavier than 1/2 ounce when casting, drifting or retrieving will unnecessarily tax the blank. A rod with a 6 to 10 pound test rating will have enough power transfer to set a #4, #2 or #1 hook; any larger size hook has too much width and also a longer tine. The line would break when transferring enough power to drive the larger hooks home. Rods with a 6 to 10 pound rating are good choices for conditions calling for light lines, small weights and bait.

2.) Reels: A Matter of Choice

Around the beginning of the Twentieth century when steelhead drift fishing was born, anglers had two styles of reels to choose from. One, they could choose a direct drive level wind. Compared to today's precision manufacturing, these level winds were crude mechanical instruments at best. Backlashes were the norm. The second choice was a single action fly reel spooled up with braided line. The angler would wear a stripping basket, literally a basket or tray that would hold coils of line out of the water or off the ground until the fisherman was ready to cast. The single action reel was the popular choice with drift fishermen of the time, as these reels, in tandem with the stripping baskets, were the easiest to use. Todays reels, however, are so well made that their use is but an afterthought.

Aside from old-timers and diehards that still use the single action reel and the "strip and flip" technique, you will see two styles of reels on steelhead rivers: level wind and spinning. When discussing spinning reels, we will be dealing with the open-face style. Closed-faced reels do not have the line capacity nor the proper drag mechanism. They may be fine for small hatchery steelhead, but if the unlucky fisherman ties into a 20 pound plus fresh native, he would need goggles to protect his eyes from exploding reel parts. It's a fact that eight out of ten anglers will employ a level wind for drift fishing. When dealing with large, powerful fish like steelhead, the level wind has more power and immediate drag and line control than a spinning reel. This statement by no means is the last word on reels, as many drift fishermen prefer spinning outfits. It is simply a matter of personal choice. Each style of reel has advantages and disadvantages that result in trade-offs in effectiveness.

Consider the following comparisons and make your own judgment. Level-wind reels take considerable practice to use effectively; spinning reels can be cast effectively by a beginner immediately. The act of reeling a spinning reel without gaining line on the spool will twist and weaken the line, which can't happen with a level wind. Spinning reels can be cast effectively from any position; level winds cannot be used in tight, brushy areas where there is no room for a back-cast. When casting level winds, there is always the possibility of a backlash; spinning reels are almost foulproof. Level winds have a better drag system due to the line coming off the spool in a straight line, instead of a 90 degree angle off the bail of a spinning reel, which increases friction. This adds drag pressure and creates a weak point in the line. Spinning reels can cast tiny, light or weight-free baits effortlessly, while some level winds require substantial weight to pull line from the spool. Spinning reels work best with light lines, 4, 6 and 8 pound tests, due to heavier monos having more memory and tending to coil. This line memory makes casting, or casting for any distance, difficult. Level winds work best with heavier monos, 10 pound test and up, because the thicker diameter lines have less tendency to backlash. When fishing the extended drift or trying to keep in contact with the bottom during a presentation, line can be fed with ease from a level wind by leaving it in free-spool or direct drive and allowing the line to slip off the reel by "feathering" the spool with the thumb. The angler has complete control over the amount of line let out, and the hook can be set immediately by clamping down on the spool. Extending a drift or keeping in the proximity of the bottom is more difficult with a spinning reel. However, with some practice you can leave the anti-reverse switch on the off position and back-reel the spinning reel to extend the drift.

These are just some of the major pros and cons of spinning and level-wind reels. Whichever style you choose, look for simplicity. In level winds, choose a reel that has a direct drive switch to allow you to pay out line and have immediate line control when a fish is in close. Stay away from all the "bass fishin'" extras, as they do nothing to help the steelheader. For a spinning reel, get one with a large capacity spool and a large, smooth drag capable of handling strong fish. Look for reels with high gear

Reels

The steelheader has two choices for drift fishing: the spinning reel (top), or the more popular level-wind (bottom).

71

ratios, such as 4.5:1, 5.2:1, and 5.6:1, for example. These high gear ratios allow you to keep up with a steelhead that has picked up the bait and is zooming right at you. Faster line retrieval means more time presenting and less time reeling between casts.

When walking the river banks, use care where you set down your reel. A few well placed grains of sand will jam a reel, either in the spool, in the handle, or worst, in the gears. When this happens, you are done for the day. When carrying a spare spool (or reel), wrap it in a layer of clear plastic wrap. This will keep sand, dirt and other assorted junk from getting into the grease or moving parts while the reel jostles around in a vest.

Whichever style you choose, a practical drift fisherman will have both styles of reels at his disposal to cover any situation encountered on the river. Keep in mind that there will always be times and places where one reel will out-perform the other.

3.) Lines: The Critical Connection

A landmark date in angling history was the patent of monofilament lines by the Du Pont Company in 1938. Although the nylon synthetic fiber was sold by the company at the time to other manufacturers for use in braided lines and fly lines, it was the start of a revolution. With the exploding popularity of the spinning reel in the mid-1950s came the demand for more castable lines. Braided nylon was too bulky, became heavy when water-soaked and needed to be stretched out before each use. When Du Pont introduced Stren (1957) and Berkely introduced Dew Flex (1958), these new monofilaments changed sportfishing like no other event in the history of the sport.

In this part of the chapter, we will be discussing mainlines, not leaders, as leaders were covered in Chapter Three. Your mainline is your working tool for drift fishing. When choosing a line, always buy the best premium quality monofilament line you can afford. High quality lines are more expensive for good reason: they are stronger and last longer. Saving a few pennies on a lower grade line will not diminish the agony of a lost trophy.

Today's steelheader has access to the best quality lines ever produced. Meteoric improvements in chemical and extruder technology have produced monofilament lines that are far better than the monos of the Elvis era. There are a dozen premium monofilaments available to the drift fisherman, and each has characteristics that help fool and land fish. The lines of today are thinner and are available in colors ranging from glowing fluorescent blue, green and gold to subtle tone browns, green, pink and clear. They have tremendous tensile strength, greater flexibility, greater knot strength, less memory and vary in stretch and limpness.

Which monofilament is right for you? If you would like to start an argument, complete with finger pointing and a five minute deliberation on the inadequacies of each other's ancestors, just bring a dozen steelheaders in a room and declare which brand of line is best. Drift fishermen will choose a line that matches where and when they fish, and if that line has served them well over the years, the confidence factor alone is reason enough not to change. For drift fishing, there are some characteristics a line must have. One, it must be a premium quality, high tensile strength line. High tensile strength means superior knot strength and abrasion resistance. These are two important features to look for in a line. The knots must be able

There are approximately a dozen premium quality monofilaments for the drift fisherman to choose. Pick the highest quality line you can afford.

to withstand the shock of hooksets and bolting steelhead, and because of the nature of drift fishing—making frequent contact with rocks—a harder finished, abrasion resistant line is necessary.

Your mainline should be slightly heavier than your leader. This will ensure that when a solid snag occurs, only the leader or the terminal outfit will be lost. Using leaders that are the same pound test, or heavier, than the mainline invites the chance to break off long sections of mainline. Besides leaving long pieces of line strung out through the prime spot in the drift, trying to break off will put an unnecessary strain on the mainline. Match your leader with mainline accordingly, such as 8 pound leader to 10 pound mainline, 10 pound leader with 12 pound mainline, etc. Do not assume that just because a line is labeled as 12 pound test that it will break at 12 pounds. Lines can vary greatly between brands. For example, some labeled at 12 pound actually break at 18. Know your brand's capacity when matching leaders with mainlines.

The second and most important characteristic of a mainline is that it must be able to be visually followed through a drift. Using a visible line allows you to see exactly where your drift is working. Natural colored lines are almost impossible to visually follow through a drift. With monos that disappear into the glare, there is no way of knowing if you are working the same spot twice. There is also no way of knowing if your terminal gear is going under an obstruction, such as a log or rocks, until it's too late. With a visible line you can work your gear as close as possible to these same obstructions (often holding spots for low water fish) without guesswork or fear of snagging. Being able to see the line will help detect light pickups. This is because many times the line will vibrate or move, giving away the presence of a steelhead, even when you cannot feel the take. Anglers who use nonvisible lines are needlessly handicapping themselves. The best color lines for drift fishing range from any of the fluorescent colors for dark days and water conditions with color or limited visibility; to clear or pink on bright days or maximum visibility conditions. Studies by fish biologists have shown conclusively that the one color line fish cannot see is pink. That is why virtually all commercial gillnets are made of pink monofilament.

One tip: you may still use bright, highly visible lines in clear water or on bright days without spooking wary steelhead, by coloring the first several feet of the mainline above the swivel/weight with a black, waterproof Magic Marker. Running the marker up and down the line a few times camouflages the fluorescent color.

Regardless of the color or brand of line you choose, be sure to replace it often: after 2 or 3 trips, or if more than 20 yards have been lost from breakoffs of reties. Regardless of the line quality, abrasion is part of the game, and playing fish (and breaking off) will stretch and weaken monofilament. Purchasing line in bulk spools not only saves money but allows you to change to fresh line often. There is no need to empty a spool each time you change your line; 80 to 100 yards of mainline is all that is required. This will save you money, and any steelhead that gets this far away from you will be long gone anyway. A smart thing to do is to fill the reel one-quarter to one-half full of backing before spooling on the mainline. Braided nylon is an excellent choice for backing, as it is much stronger than the mainline and will last for years before it needs replacing. Use the blood knot to join the mainline and the backing.

Be sure to check your mainline every so often for abrasion and nicks. Run the line between your thumb and forefinger. If it feels rough, clip off that section and retie. Nicked, rough line will lessen the pound test greatly and cost you fish! Keep your reels and line spools out of hot car trunks, as well as out of direct sunlight. Rods hanging in the back of the window in the pickup may look stylish, but hot sun and UV rays damage monofilament. The best way to store line is in a cool, dark area.

Using the lightest practical mainline for the conditions is the first consideration for the drift fisherman, but keep this in mind. When practicing catch and release, the sooner a fish is landed, the better chance it has for survival. Long, drawn-out battles with too light a line exhaust a fish and allow lactic acid to build in its muscle tissue. This can kill a steelhead. By using the heaviest possible mainline and leader, you may play a steelhead with more control and land it quicker.

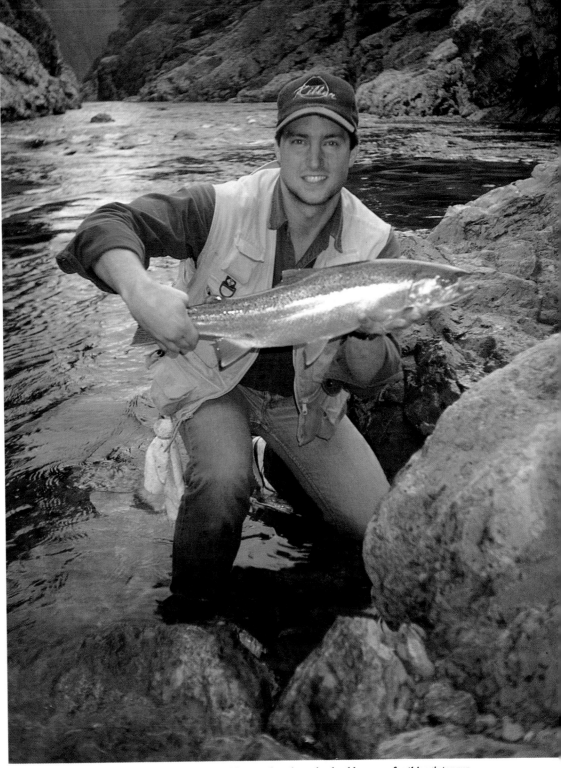
David Kilhefner used a "visible" line to guide a roe bag through a boulder maze for this winter-run.

4.) Setting Up a Vest

When Lee Wulff patented the first fishing vest (circa 1940), it was intended to make carrying fly fishing paraphernalia easier and more convenient while wading rivers. I don't think Lee had any idea that his invention would be the featured carry-all system of today's steelhead drift fishermen. The vest is an absolute necessity for the bank or even the boat angler. Carrying around a tackle box is much too cumbersome, inconvenient, and can be stolen easily. The fishing vest carries all items for drift fishing close at hand, secure and out of the way.

When setting up a vest for drift fishing, it is important to have all the right gear, and the right amount of gear. Too heavy a vest can lead to fatigue, as a bulging vest is clumsy and restricts movement. However, not carrying enough gear can lead to going home a lot earlier than planned. The following is a suggested list in alphabetical order of 20 items that a drift fisherman needs for a day's steelheading.

Bags (plastic zip-loc style): Any item that needs to stay dry can be placed in these clear bags for protection and easy identification. These bags make good containers for rolled-up discarded monofilament, as they keep the line from unraveling in the pocket and will hold skein eggs from hatchery fish.

Bait threader: Carry one for sand shrimp, prawns and worms. See Chapter Five for more information on bait threaders.

Bait towel: Hang a small, face-type towel on the bottom front of the vest. There is usually a small loop of material on the vest that the towel can be attached to. The towel will keep your hands free of borax, egg juice or any other lovely excrements from steelhead baits and keep your reel and rod free of the same goop. The bait towel is a great alternative to rinsing your hands in frigid water on cold winter mornings.

Beads: For knot protectors on sliding weights, and for bearings on spinning drift bobbers. Use 3 to 4 mm red beads for low to normal conditions, and 5mm glow beads for high or restricted visibility conditions. Place a few dozen of each in a small, flat, clear plastic box, or in a small diameter plastic tube that takes up even less space. Note that clear plastic containers allow for instant identification when searching through a vest pocket. Save empty hook boxes, they make excellent containers.

Drift bobbers: You would need a caddie with a backpack to carry all the possible colors, sizes and styles of drift bobbers. When at home or at your vehicle, prepare a clear, compartmented box (clear fly boxes are perfect for carrying drift bobbers) with pre-determined colors, styles and sizes that will match probable water conditions. This way you can avoid carrying a large bulky assortment of bobbers. Regardless of the styles you choose, pack at least twenty to thirty in two different sizes.

Floats: As was discussed in Chapter Four, a float adds access to holding water when the bank angler is restricted. Carry at least two of the dink style.

Glasses (Polarized): As important to the bank angler as any other piece of equipment. Polarized glasses help you four ways. One, in low, clear water conditions they allow you to spot holding

Tacoma angler Mike Cronen found all the right combinations in his vest to catch this "springer."

steelhead and give you the opportunity to cast to these sighted fish that might be passed by or accidentally spooked. Two, they allow you to see underwater obstructions that could hold fish or eat your terminal gear. Three, you will be able to identify holding water and pockets that may have been hidden by glare. Finally, the glasses provide a safety factor by protecting your eyes from glare, which causes squinting and eventually a headache. They allow you to wade safely; they keep brush, tree limbs and undergrowth from lashing across your eyes, and protect them from damaging UV rays. You can purchase a good pair for under twenty dollars. There are more expensive polarized glasses on the market, but they perform no better than cheaper ones.

Journal: The journal is your ticket to future successful steelheading trips. Anything that occurs on the river is important; fishless days can provide as much information on steelhead behavior as fish filled ones. Any or all information about the date, water temperature, style/size/color of drift bobber, type of holding water and so on. All can be lost if you rely totally on memory. By taking a few minutes during the day's fishing to enter notes in a pocket journal, you can document steelhead behavior, run timing, best baits for conditions and a host of other things that would be hazy if trusted to memory. Over the years you will see patterns develop that you may plan trips around, and you will find that the journal will rarely let you down. The chart below is an example of a pocket journal that you may

copy and carry with you. By quickly checking a few boxes and scribbling important notes, you will have enough information to be transferred to a more detailed journal at home. True, keeping a journal involves a lot of writing, but every bit saved is valuable information for future trips. Store the pocket journal in a zip-lock bag.

Knife: For cleaning hatchery steelhead; for use as an emergency screwdriver or a host of other reasons (like cutting out a bird's nest) to have one.

Leaders: Carry a minimum of 12 to 16 leaders, pre-tied, yarn added and pre-sharpened to save time on the water. Bring two different pound tests and hook sizes to match probable river conditions. The round "Pip's"-style leader housings fit nicely into vest pockets and protect the line and bumper knots from abrasion while jostling around in the pocket. From 24 to 32 leaders will fit into one container, and you may want to color code the different pound tests by using two separate colors of yarn for immediate identification.

License (and pen): Store and carry your license in your vest, as it will be easier to get at than if buried in a wallet under neoprene waders. Keep license and pen in a clear zip-lock bag to protect them from moisture.

Lighter: The cheap, disposable type will suffice. Lighters are essential for melting ends of slinky cord or starting a fire on cold mornings. Store the lighter in a zip-lock bag to be sure of a dry flint when you need it.

Pliers: The number one tool of the drift fisherman. Pliers have dozens of important uses including cutting, pinching and perforating lead, removing hooks from steelhead, to bending back or offsetting hooks and pinching down barbs. The needle-nose style with built in cutters are the most practical, with specially designed ones for lead use the best. To make sure you never lose your pliers or drop them accidentally into the water, add a 1-1/2 foot length of surgical tubing to the handle. Peel three-quarters of an inch off the vinyl coating on one of the handles and slip one end of the tubing onto it. Tie the loose end of the tubing to the "D" ring on the breast pocket.

Reel (spare): Nothing ever goes as planned; even gear malfunctions happen despite the most careful preparation. Since there is no way to predict or prevent glitches, you must carry a spare reel. Level-wind fishermen know the time lost from a bird's nest; and anyone that has had a bail mechanism fail on a spinning reel knows the frustration. Without a spare, you are done for the day. You may also want to change to the spare reel for its lighter/heavier test line. Keep the spare reel in a zip-lock bag, or wrap it in clear food wrap to keep dirt and lint out of the grease and gears.

Rubber bands: To keep boxes of drift bobbers, swivels, etc., from opening and spilling their contents inside the vest pockets. They are perfect for holding the rod together when breaking it down for traveling or moving through brushy spots.

Scents: Carry one scent in oil form in an injector bottle, and one small jar of paste scent to match baits or for use in limited visibility conditions. (Chapter Five has more information on scents.)

Pocket Journal

Date:_____ Time:_____
❑ Steelhead ❑ Salmon ❑ Trout Other:_____

Water Conditions-

Temp	❑ 33-39	❑ 40-43	❑ 44-49	❑ 50-53
	❑ 54-57	❑ 58-62	❑ 63-67	❑ 68+___
Clarity	❑ 1-2 ft.	❑ 2-6 ft.	❑ 6 ft. +	
Surface	❑ smooth	❑ lt. brkn.	❑ hvy. brkn.	
Depth	❑ 104 ft.	❑ 4-8 ft.	❑ 8-12 ft.	❑ 12 ft.+
Speed	❑ slow	❑ medium	❑ fast	

Water Type-
❑ head ❑ run ❑ tail ❑ rapid ❑ fast ❑ pocket ❑ riffle ❑ break ❑ Other:_____

Lighting/Weather-
❑ sunlight ❑ bright/direct ❑ indirect ❑ shade ❑ light clouds ❑ heavy clouds ❑ wind
Weather notes:_____
_____
_____
_____

Rig/Presentation
rig:_____
❑ upstream ❑ downstream ❑ across ❑ bottom
❑ mid-depth ❑ surface

Scissors (or clippers): For trimming line after tying knots; for cutting slinky cord; or trimming yarn and roe bags.

Sharpeners: As important as any other piece of drift fishing gear, a sharpener is an absolute necessity for touching up dulled hooks. Carry a fine, flat-surfaced diamond type for smaller hooks, and a coarse diamond or metal file for larger hooks. Remember: with dull hooks, you will lose fish.

Swivels: You need two different styles for drift fishing: a #5 or #7 barrel, and a #7 (large) and a #10 snap swivel. With these two types of swivels, you can rig lead and slinkies either sliding or solid tie. Black is the preferred color for swivels in clearer water. When the water is colored, brass will suffice. Carry a couple dozen of each type and size in a small clear plastic box.

Swivels

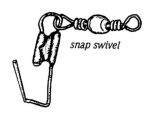

snap swivel

barrel swivel

Tape: A roll of black vinyl electrician's tape is the answer for on-the-river emergency repairs, such as a broken rod tip or loose reel seat. Black vinyl tape makes a strong, flexible mend that allows you to keep fishing after a mishap.

Thermometer: One of the bank fisherman's essentials. Knowing water temperature will not only tell you what kind of holding water to look for, but also help you choose the proper drift fishing technique.

Weights: Choose which style of weighting system will match the water/river bottom conditions before you leave home. To carry enough styles and amounts of weight to cover all possibilities would take too much space, and add considerable poundage to the vest. Select one or two weighting systems and carry enough for the day's fishing. Knowing the river structure before you fish will aid you greatly in selecting weighting systems and how much to pack along. An option if you choose to fish slinkies is to make one long slinky, then cut it to size after checking water conditions. The long slinky and all lead may be carried loose in a pocket, while pre-made slinkies may be snapped onto a large ring above the breast pocket with snap swivels already attached.

Is there anything left off this list? I'm sure there must be a few items each angler cannot function without. With all this drift fishing gear packed in the vest, it should weigh approximately six pounds.

When choosing a vest, again we are confronted with different tastes and ideas concerning which design works best for the indi-vidual. This is fine, but there is one point to remember. Try to purchase a vest that has the majority of its larger main pockets equipped with zipper closures. Velcro pocket closures can open at inopportune times, such as when you're leaning over the water or being rubbed by brush. How you load all gear into the vest is also a matter of personal choice. Each drift fisherman has a preferred place in the vest for each item. The only rule to follow when loading the pockets is to keep the vest in balance. Putting all the heavy items, such as weights, on one side will put you off-balance and force one arm and shoulder to work harder. This can add to fatigue after hiking all day. Be sure to spread items evenly to keep the vest hanging squarely on the shoulders.

A final note: Keep a checklist for your vest so you don't forget anything. Even if one of the items listed here is forgotten, it could mean the day is over before it really starts. Make a separate list for high water, normal water and low/clear conditions. One more thing. Don't forget your camera. You will want a photo of that beautiful native steelhead before you release it!

5.) Waders and Other Waterproof Wear

Serious steelheaders, regardless of time of year, cannot fish effectively if they are soaking wet and miserable. Believe me, there are more ways than one to absorb water while on the river. When you are wet, the last thing you want to do is spend another hour shivering. Steelheading in wet clothing is uncomfortable. Other than those rare summer days when the temperature soars above 80 degrees and the prospect of getting wet has an appeal, time on a steelhead river often translates to rain, wet bushes and the necessity of wading to access the proper position on the holding water. The angler must be outfitted to endure cold rivers and whatever else Mother Nature throws at you. The steelheader must rely on waders and raingear to stay dry and comfortable.

For the boat angler, calf-high or hip boots are fine. Other than stepping out of the boat into a foot of water when going ashore, or sloshing around in a few inches of rainwater in the boat itself, these will be the only encounters with wading. For rainy days, or for just keeping your seat dry, a good quality pair of rain pants serves the boat fisherman perfectly. Buy a pair that are large enough to fit easily over hip or calf-high boots and allow ease of mobility.

For the bank angler, needs are different and a bit more complicated. For rivers that are too large, or the bank configuration does not allow wading, hip boots or calf-high waterproof boots are adequate. However, these situations will be the only ones where this footwear is acceptable. For all other bank fishing situations encountered, however, the steelheader must own a good quality pair of chest high or waist high waders. Hip boots are an invitation for wet feet. If it happens to rain hard, or the angler wades in just a bit too deep (which is inevitable), the boots will fill up. Nice. Remember, hip boots are better suited for washing the car than for serious bank angling.

What kind of waders are available? You have two choices: lightweight or neoprene, in boot foot and stocking foot. Boot foot waders have the boot already built onto the wader, while stocking foot waders need a wading shoe. Each has advantages and disadvantages, depending on the type of bank angling you are doing

Neoprene is the warmest, most comfortable and flexible style of wader available to the steelheader.

vary in price each material will keep you cool and dry. In cold, or even early morning wading in warm weather, neoprene waders are the choice, and are the most popular wader seen on the rivers today. Neoprene is the choice over ancient rubber waders because of their light weight and flexibility. Anyone who has spent time hiking in the old heavy rubber suits of armor can really appreciate neoprene. Walking in rubber waders felt like your knees were tied together. Unlike rubber, neoprenes fit snugly and stretch to your every movement. Climbing over logs and boulders is no longer an Olympic event with neoprene. They are also much warmer.

Neoprene waders are available in two thicknesses: 3mm and 5mm. The 3mm is the most flexible, is a bit lighter and can be worn without too much discomfort in warm weather if you happen to be wading in glacial rivers. The 5mm is the warmest wader you can purchase and is excellent for cold weather and extended wading. For either the 3 or 5mm neoprene wader, select ones with added knee pads. When climbing, kneeling on rocks to release fish, or rinsing your hands, etc., knee pads are a welcome addition. If the pair of stocking foot neoprenes you have chosen do not come with built-in gravel guards, buy a pair and use them, they will not only protect the feet from abrasion but also add life to the waders.

With wading shoes, sneakers or built-in boots, you'll want the bottoms of the soles to match the river bottom. If you will be doing more wading than walking, felt soles are the choice. Felt gives you traction on algae-covered rocks. For wading extremely slippery rivers (the North Fork of the Umpqua is a grand example, with ice-slick shelves making up the majority of the bottom) add aluminum cleats to the felt for added traction and safety. If you are doing more hiking than wading and only stepping into the water occasionally, then the plain rubber bottom of the sneaker or wading shoe will be fine, as the rubber cleats give better traction on rock faces and dirt than felt.

You will also want a plain rubber bottom if you are fishing in the snow. Snow sticks to felt like Velcro, and you will grow several inches with each step. Snow buildup on the bottom of felt soles is extremely uncomfortable when trying to walk. Snow will not stick to rubber.

When using a wading shoe, wear an oversized sock over the wader bootie. It will protect the foot from wear and tear, and will help keep rocks and gravel out of the shoes.

When purchasing waders, choose ones that fit well but not too snugly, and be sure that the inseam is high enough in the crotch so you have freedom of movement to step up and over objects. If you cannot find a pair that fits properly, many compa-

and time of year. Boot foot waders are the choice in cold weather, due to the insulation of the boot, and the fact there is also room inside the boot for a pair of wool socks for added warmth. If wading constantly and doing minimal walking, the boot foot will keep you comfortable and warm. If you will be doing a lot of hiking, then stocking foot waders are the choice. They are more comfortable on your feet after walking for some distance and provide better stability on rocks. I have found that when hiking all day, a pair of high top sneakers are fifty times more comfortable than wading shoes. The stocking foot wader, however, is more constrictive around the foot, limiting circulation. They do not keep your feet warm if you must wade or sit for long periods in cold weather. On the other hand, stocking foot waders are easier and quicker to dry than boot foot, as they may be turned inside-out. Boot foot waders can only be rolled down to the boot tops.

For warm weather, lightweight waders are the choice, because they are thin and non-insulated. This makes them especially comfortable for spring/summer steelheading. Lightweight waders are made of rubber, nylon and Gore-Tex, and though they

If you do a considerable amount of hiking/walking in your waders, consider a pair of high-top sneakers in place of wading shoes for extra mobility and comfort.

wading in our fast-flowing steelhead rivers.

In steelhead country, however, water also comes from above. Rain is part of the deal, especially in winter months. Staying dry and warm requires good raingear. There are several qualities to look for when purchasing raingear. First, make sure the rain jacket you choose is large enough so it does not restrict arm movement in any direction. Tight-fitting rain jackets are downright uncomfortable, and limited movement adds to fatigue. Buy a rain jacket that allows you to wear several layers of warm clothing underneath, and still have total freedom of movement. Get one with a built-in hood, large enough to totally cover the brim of a fishing cap beneath. The large hood will keep rain from coming in the sides and trickling down your neck. The hood should have an adjustable drawstring to keep the hood up during windy periods. A steelheader's rain jacket should have sleeve ends that are elastic or adjustable to close snugly around the wrist. This feature keeps rain from running down your arm and accumulating at the elbow.

The rain jacket should hang down no longer than just past the waist. If you do any wading deeper than the thighs, a longer raincoat will catch in the current and throw you off balance. With chest high or waist high waders any rain jacket longer than the waist is unnecessary. However, a longer rain jacket may be desired when walking the banks with hip or calf-high boots, as the longer tails will keep your rear and upper legs dry.

The color of your raingear, like that of any other part of the steelheader's clothing, should be subtle and natural. Bank fishermen especially should wear raingear in greens, browns or camo so as not to spook fish in clear or small water. Bright yellow and orange should be worn only by road workers. Besides scaring steelhead, you will save yourself some verbal abuse from other anglers by not wearing gaudy clothing near their water!

Good quality waterproof gear, waders and rain wear, will allow you to spend hours of dry, warm and comfortable fishing on the river, even in the most inclement weather.

nies now offer custom-fitted neoprene and lightweight waders. They are a bit more expensive, but comfort is of paramount importance when selecting waders. Personally, I wear waders for all steelhead fishing, bank or boat. Neoprenes keep me warm and dry when sitting in a drift boat all day.

A word of caution when wading. The best rule to remember to avoid trouble is never wade in swift flowing current deeper than your crotch. Once you go past this point, you become buoyant and can easily lose your footing. Use common sense when

Staying dry and warm by wearing quality raingear allows you to drift fish in relative comfort, even during rain squalls such as this one.

How To Release Steelhead

Play and release steelhead as rapidly as your gear allows. A fish played with a soft hand over a long period of time may suffer from lactic acid buildup in the muscle tissue, or die from over-exertion.

Keep the steelhead in the water as much as possible. Three to 6 inches of water is an adequate cushion. Out of the water, a steelhead's weight is many times what it is in the water.

If you want a photo, gently cradle the fish with one hand on the bottom of the fish, just behind the pectoral fins, and firmly grasp the wrist of the tail with the other. Do not allow the fish to flop on rocks or sand, as this may cause internal damage and remove the steelhead's protective slime coat.

Keep fingers out of gill plates, as ripped gill rakers will cause the fish to bleed to death. Remove the hook as gently and rapidly as possible with needle-nose pliers or hemostats. If the steelhead is deeply hooked, cut the leader and leave the hook in the fish. Its natural body acids will eventually dissolve the hook.

After your photo, hold the fish upright in modestly flowing water facing upstream. Allow the fish to catch its breath, and when revived, it will start to struggle and show renewed strength. When the fish can swim normally, let go of the tail wrist and let it return to fulfill its destiny.

Releasing a Fish

2. Hold the fish upright in the current to allow oxygen to circulate through the gills.

1. Cradle steelhead in the shallow, slow-flowing portion of the drift where it was caught.

3. When the steelhead is revived and starts to show strength, let go of the tail wrist and let it swim away.

79

Index